Victory in the
Valleys of Life

This is a complete list of books by Charles L. Allen since he became a Revell author in 1951.

GOD'S PSYCHIATRY
THE TOUCH OF THE MASTER'S HAND
ALL THINGS ARE POSSIBLE THROUGH PRAYER
WHEN YOU LOSE A LOVED ONE
WHEN THE HEART IS HUNGRY
THE TWENTY-THIRD PSALM
THE TEN COMMANDMENTS
THE LORD'S PRAYER
THE BEATITUDES
TWELVE WAYS TO SOLVE YOUR PROBLEMS
HEALING WORDS
THE LIFE OF CHRIST
PRAYER CHANGES THINGS
THE SERMON ON THE MOUNT
LIFE MORE ABUNDANT
THE CHARLES L. ALLEN TREASURY (Charles L. Wallis)
ROADS TO RADIANT LIVING
RICHES OF PRAYER
IN QUEST OF GOD'S POWER
WHEN YOU GRADUATE (with Mouzon Biggs)
THE MIRACLE OF LOVE
THE MIRACLE OF HOPE
THE MIRACLE OF THE HOLY SPIRIT
CHRISTMAS IN OUR HEARTS (with Charles L. Wallis)
CANDLE, STAR AND CHRISTMAS TREE (with Charles L. Wallis)
WHEN CHRISTMAS CAME TO BETHLEHEM (with Charles L. Wallis)
CHRISTMAS (with Charles L. Wallis)
WHAT I HAVE LIVED BY
YOU ARE NEVER ALONE
PERFECT PEACE
HOW TO INCREASE YOUR SUNDAY-SCHOOL ATTENDANCE (with Mildred Parker)
THE SECRET OF ABUNDANT LIVING
VICTORY IN THE VALLEYS OF LIFE

Victory in the Valleys of Life

Charles L. Allen

Fleming H. Revell Company
Old Tappan, New Jersey

Library of Congress Cataloging in Publication Data
Allen, Charles Livingstone, date
  Victory in the valleys of life.
    1. Consolation.   I. Title.
BV4905.2.A397   248.4′87606   81-10619
ISBN 0-8007-1271-4   AACR2

TO:
Marvin Key Collie, Jr.,
Houston, Texas,
who gives unusually outstanding leadership and love to his family,
his church, the legal profession, and his community

Contents

Acknowledgment

I wish to express my appreciation to Mrs. Constance Ward, my secretary, for her most valuable help in preparing this manuscript.

"Yea, Though I Walk Through the Valley"

1

"Have You Ever Walked Through the Valley?"

I was visiting with a friend of mine in Jerusalem, Mr. Emil Abubayeh. He has lived in Israel for more than seventy years and is one of the most respected and successful businessmen there. We were talking about the country of Israel and all of the great people who have lived there. Somehow the name of David came up, and suddenly he asked me this question, "Have you ever walked through the Valley of the Shadow of Death?"

I began talking about the fact that sooner or later all of us have difficult experiences in life and eventually every person will walk through some valley. "Oh, no," he said, "I mean have you literally visited that valley here in Israel?"

I told him that I was familiar with the Twenty-third Psalm, but I said I realized that David was referring to an experience in life, not a real place.

Mr. Abubayeh explained to me that it *is* a real place and suggested that, the next morning, he come by my hotel to get me and carry me to visit that valley. I can hardly describe my excitement.

One of the greatest joys I have is going with groups to visit the Holy Land. I have been there twenty times, and each time it is a new and an exciting experience. However, in all my trips, never once had I ever heard any reference to that valley.

Since I am not a very good photographer, I asked Mrs. Mildred Parker, the codirector of our tours, and one or two others to go with us. The pictures on the jacket of this book are some that Mrs. Parker took that morning.

As we drove along, Mr. Abubayeh explained that in the very early spring the shepherds led their sheep from the fields around Bethlehem, down to the fields in the vicinity of Jericho. There they sought the grass which had come out of the ground several weeks earlier. To reach the fields it was almost essential that they go through this valley.

I really thought we would never get to the fields ourselves, because we went over the roughest road I have ever seen. At least half a dozen times all of us got out of the car, and sometimes we even had to push our vehicle over certain bad places in the road. During the ride, the scenery became more exciting. The hills and valleys in the distance were beautiful. Finally we went over a hill, and suddenly there it was: the Valley of the Shadow of Death!

Mr. Abubayeh stopped the car; we got out, and for more than thirty minutes we stood, feasting our eyes on this magnificently beautiful sight. The valley winds its way through high mountains on each side. We could see caves on the sides of the mountains; here, Mr. Abubayeh explained, the shepherds would bed down their sheep for the night. The caves were welcome places to rest and shelter from the cold weather.

He further explained that in biblical days many people travelled through the valley, going from the Bethlehem area to the Jericho area and back. Oftentimes robbers would bed down in those caves, waiting for someone to pass by. He reminded us of the story of the man who was going from Jerusalem down to Jericho, ". . . and fell among thieves, which stripped him of his raiment, and wounded him, and departed, leaving him half dead" (Luke 10:30). As the story shows, these thieves could be vicious and murderous. The shepherds also faced the threat of wild animals, especially wolves, who would attack the sheep. As a boy David remembered how both a lion and a bear attacked sheep that he was shepherding (1 Samuel 17:34). Those attacks might have come in this very place.

Though this was the most feasible route from Bethlehem to Jericho and back, the valley was a very dangerous place.

I cannot describe my excitement as I stood on the rim of that valley and gazed down it; we got in the car and drove to the very bottom. I spent five hours walking through that valley. The Twenty-third Psalm became more alive to me than ever before. I noticed the countless little green patches as I walked along, some of which were not more than fifteen feet in diameter. I could picture a flock of sheep lying down in one of those beautiful little grassy spots.

Down through the valley flows a beautiful, clear stream that supplies Jerusalem with some of its water. I could imagine little sheep being frightened by that swift-running, rocky stream. Every so often, though, I would come upon a beautiful pond, and it was easy to understand the phrase ". . . he leadeth me beside the still waters."

As I walked through that valley, I understood what it meant to have the protecting care of both a loving and a capable shepherd: one who carried a rod and a staff, one who could care for the sheep if it cut its leg on a sharp rock, one who could guide the sheep through the various paths all the way through the valley.

As we reluctantly left that beautiful place, I realized that I had literally done what David said, "Yea, though I walk through the valley of the shadow of death . . . ." I thought about how, eventually, in one way or another, every person walks through that valley.

On the way back to Jerusalem, we went through Anathoth, the town where Jeremiah was born. I thought about the Weeping Prophet and about how many other people have wept in the valley.

2

What Causes Fear?

The phrase from the Twenty-third Psalm, "the valley of the shadow of death," does not refer to the experience of death. Literally the words used to describe the valley originally meant "dark shadows" rather than "the shadow of death." Although David may have included death in his thoughts, the passage refers to much more.

In the dark ravines of that valley near Jerusalem, there were lurking places for ferocious beasts and robbers. Some felt it was a place of evil spirits.

This valley became a symbol of the circumstances in life that give rise to fear. When David says, ". . . I will fear no evil . . . ," the word he used for "death" was the same one used for "evil," or whatever might cause fear. It symbolizes that which deprives either sheep or people of the good things in life and the "pursuit of happiness."

Slowly and painfully our little car made its way up the steep valley road. As we reached the rim, I said to Mr. Abubayeh, "Let's stop and get out and take one more look." I stood looking across the valley that I thought only existed in the Twenty-third Psalm. Suddenly, seeing the land David described, I was confronted with the reality of the valleys in our lives.

When I think of that valley, I do not only remember the beauty, but also the pitfalls, the precipices, the beasts and robbers, and all the evil. What a vivid comparison to life experience! I am reminded of the dismal words of the Psalmist, "Like sheep they are laid in the grave; death shall feed on them . . ." (Psalms 49:14). However, I also consider the glorious words written centuries later: "The people which sat in darkness saw great light; and to them which sat in the region and shadow of death light is sprung up" (Matthew 4:16).

3

"He Keeps Playing When He Is Hurt"

I was watching a football game on the television and was particularly struck by a comment by the announcer. One of the players had taken a hard lick. He was obviously in pain, lying on the ground. I thought the coach would surely send in a substitute and take this man out of the game. Instead the player slowly got up and went back to the huddle. The announcer said, "He keeps playing when he is hurt."

The truth is, a lot of people play when they are hurt, and there are a lot of ways to be hurt. To be hurt in a football stadium with 60,000 people looking on is rather dramatic, but a lot of people hurt when it isn't a bit exciting. Some of the hardest valleys to walk through are dullness, boredom, and emptiness. When the hurt is exciting, it may be easier to keep on playing. There is challenge in the risk and adventure of life, and we keep going, even though we are hurt. But when people are simply living and there is nothing to be excited about, we really do begin to feel the boredom. People who face this valley begin to fear rejection and tend to stay hidden.

When life has lost its excitement, we have a feeling of emptiness. We lose all purpose and motivation, and we may give ourselves to nothing outside the circle of self-interest. We reach the point where we do not dream of any mountains to climb, any battles to win or any desires to be satisfied. It is then that many people seek to escape life through day-dreaming, alcohol, drugs, imagined sickness, and even suicide.

On the other hand, another common escape for the empty, bored, gloomy life is ceaseless activity. Instead of becoming alcoholics some people become workaholics. They live their lives purely on the material level, forgetting all of the beauty and joys that might be. Someone wrote these words:

For those who seek the answer
In houses, lands and rings,
Will someday find their empty lives
Just as empty filled with things.

One can be successful in accumulating things and still find nothing in life really worth living for.

One of the authors who has inspired me through the years is T. S. Eliot. In act 1 of *The Elder Statesman* he wrote:

LORD CLARENDON: I have not the slightest longing for the
     life I have left—
Only fear of the emptiness before me.
If I had the energy to work myself to death
How gladly would I face death! but waiting, simply waiting,
With no desire to act, yet a loathing of inaction.
A fear of the vacuum, and no desire to fill it.
It's just like sitting in an empty waiting room
In a railroad station or a branch line,
After the last train comes, after all the other passengers
Have left and the booking office has closed
And the porters have gone.

We frequently hear such expressions as, "I've got the blues," or, "Every day feels like Monday," or, "I have been in the dumps for days," and on and on. There are many reasons for being in this valley, but the main reason is that one feels unworthy, inadequate, and eventually completely lacking in confidence. This leads one to become riddled by fear.

In *Pilgrim's Progress,* Bunyan referred to "the slough of despond." In the army there is a term *operational fatigue.* The psychiatrist uses a word *neurosis.* The great Martin Luther once found himself caught in a mood of despair, and he cried out, "I am sick of life, if that is what you call it." The Psalmist described this feeling best, "Why art thou cast down, O my soul?" (Psalms 42:5).

4

"Yet Trouble Came," Said Job

"Yet trouble came" (Job 3:26). Sooner or later, every person can say those words with Job. In his book, *The Meaning of Suffering,* Dr. Ralph W. Sockman said that there are three types of trouble:

1. The trouble we can avoid
2. The trouble we cannot avoid
3. The trouble we must not avoid

The Trouble We Can Avoid

Much of the trouble in our lives we bring on ourselves. One of my dearest friends recently stepped off a curb, fell, and broke his leg. In talking to me about it, he simply said, "I didn't watch my step." The idea of "watching your step" is not unfamiliar to any of us. Again and again, because of our thoughtlessness or carelessness, we get hurt.

Recently I was driving to another city for a speaking engagement. As I went through a small town, I happened to glance in my rear-view mirror and saw a car behind me with its lights flashing. I pulled over to the curb, and the policeman explained to me that I was exceeding the speed limit. He gave me a ticket and said that I could mail in a check and pay the fine. I had nobody to blame but myself. I broke the law, and I paid for it. I promised myself the next time I drive through that particular town, I will be more careful. The truth is, I needed to promise myself that, whenever I am driving, I will be careful. Most of the accidents on our highways and in our homes could be avoided just by thinking.

Much of the trouble in our lives has roots in our own desires. Modern science and psychology are finally catching on to the principles that major religions have taught for thousands of years.

Jesus was criticized for the fact that he and his disciples associated with evil people. He was also asked, ". . . Why do the disciples of John and of the Pharisees fast, but thy disciples fast not?" (Mark 2:18). There were those who felt that to be good you had to be an ascetic. That simply is not true. We are made to live with each other and enjoy each other. However our associations can be destroyed by addictions to pleasure, food, money, power, prestige, drugs, or alcohol. There is such a thing as living under control. Much of the trouble that comes into a human life comes because a person loses self-control. We need to use common sense. We need to hear the advice of others. We need to study the eternal principles of human living. It has been well said, "The Ten Commandments are not the Ten Suggestions."

The Trouble We Cannot Avoid

On the other hand, much of the trouble that comes into our lives we cannot avoid. Blaming ourselves is not the answer. When Moses was on the mountain, receiving the Ten Commandments, God spoke of ". . . visiting the iniquity of the fathers upon the children unto the third and fourth generation . . ." (Exodus 20:5). Some of the troubles that come into human lives are because of parents. One of the major sins of our society is abused children. But children can be abused in many ways. Sometimes we inherit troubles because of the actions of our forefathers for generations back, but we cannot help this part of the growing pains of civilization.

Many of our troubles that we cannot help are caused by our children. The fact that parents love their children makes them vulnerable to be hurt. I do not know who said it, but I think this is wonderfully true, "You are only as happy as your unhappiest child."

When we think of trouble, we think of all of the natural disasters: earthquakes, cyclones, floods, droughts. These cannot be avoided, and we do not blame ourselves for them.

Time and again in life, we are suddenly shocked at something that is completely beyond our understanding. We cannot explain why one person has cancer and another doesn't. We do not know all the reasons why one fifty-year-old man will die of a sudden heart attack and another man will live to be eighty. Nobody can explain why some children insist on being prodigal sons and daughters. There are people who feel there is no place left for them in this world; they feel completely useless and left out. Yet they tried to live life as they felt they should. Someone has said it in a way that I like very much: "Some people feel they have reached the end of their possible."

When we think of trouble, we think of adversity. However, we need to remind ourselves that adversity is not always our enemy. Some years ago I read a book entitled, *The Way of All Flesh,* by Samuel Butler. I copied this memorable sentence out of that book: "Adversity, if a man is set down to it by degrees, is more supportable with equanimity by most people than any great property arrived at in a single lifetime." I have lived long enough to know that sometimes good fortune can be our downfall.

The Trouble We Must Not Avoid

There is that third type of trouble: the trouble we must not avoid. When you go to Westminster Abbey in London, you can find the grave of William Wilberforce. He was a powerful man in the affairs of England. Yet he was a very small and sickly man, physically. For many years he took opium under a doctor's orders, just to keep himself going; but he had the courage and the strength never to increase his dosage of opium. He was the master of his medicine. It would have been so easy for William Wilberforce to have said, "A man no bigger than I, who is sick, cannot afford to be involved in the problems and troubles of my society." But he never said it. It is now generally accepted that he was the person most responsible for the abolition of England's slave trade. Some have said of him that because of his own pain, he became sensitive to the needs of other suffering people.

As we read the story of the Good Samaritan and condemn those who "pass by on the other side," we are inspired to follow in the footsteps of the Samaritan. The Bible does not say he was *good.* As men and women have read that story, down through the centuries, our civilization has given him the title of *good.* We have come to believe that it is good to become involved in the needs and hurts of the world.

I have spent no less than a hundred nights in a hotel on the Mount of Olives. Just below that hotel is a little chapel, built at the spot where it was believed that Jesus beheld the city and wept over it (Luke 19:41). Just below is the Garden of Gethsemane. I cannot count the times that I have stood at my window in the hotel and looked down upon the garden and asked the question, "Why did Jesus stop there? Why did He not keep on walking?" Just beyond the other side of that hotel is Bethany. I have often felt that if He had just walked on over the hill, to the home of Mary and Martha, the soldiers would never have found Him. From there He could have gone back to the shores of Galilee and lived His life in peace and quiet and joy.

Frequently I have asked people on my tours in the Holy Land to tell me their moment of greatest inspiration. I get many answers, but for my own answer, there is no question. I am most touched by the rock where it is believed that Jesus knelt in the Garden of Gethsemane; there He prayed, "Father, if thou be willing, remove this cup from me: nevertheless not my will, but thine, be done" (Luke 22:42).

Some years ago, I was the minister of the Grace United Methodist Church in Atlanta, Georgia. I loved that church, and I loved the people there who gave me so much in trust and support. While I was there, we put new windows in the church. One of the windows shows our Lord kneeling in Gethsemane. I said to the artist, "In this window I want the entire experience pictured." He wondered what I meant. I explained to him that in most pictures of Jesus praying in Gethsemane, He is there alone, but that is not the case. Then I read him these words, "And there appeared an angel unto him from heaven, strengthening him" (Luke 22:43). He put the angel in the picture; in the same way, we must put the angel in our picture.

Sometimes when I get a bit discouraged, I turn and read these words of Paul's to the Corinthians:

> Five times I have received at the hands of the Jews the forty lashes less one. Three times I have been beaten with rods; once I was stoned. Three times I have been shipwrecked; a night and a day I have been adrift at sea; on frequent journeys, in danger from rivers, danger from rob-

bers, danger from my own people, danger from Gentiles, danger in the city, danger in the wilderness, danger at sea, danger from false brethren; in toil and hardship, through many a sleepless night, in hunger and thirst, often without food, in cold and exposure. And, apart from other things, there is the daily pressure upon me of my anxiety for all the churches. Who is weak, and I am not weak? Who is made to fall, and I am not indignant?

2 Corinthians 11:24–29 RSV

Here is a cry of need that should touch the heart of each of us:

I Was Hungry

I was hungry and you formed a humanities club and discussed my hunger. Thank you.

I was imprisoned and you crept off quietly to your chapel and prayed for my release.

I was naked and in your mind you debated the morality of my appearance.

I was sick and you knelt and thanked God for your health.

I was homeless and you preached to me of the spiritual shelter of the love of God.

I was lonely and you left me alone to pray for me.

You seem so holy, so close to God. But I'm still very hungry and lonely and cold.

SOURCE UNKNOWN

There are some troubles we must not avoid.

I wonder if Paul ever walked through the Valley of the Shadow of Death? We do not know, but we do know he walked through the valley as a minister of the Lord Jesus Christ.

There are times when every honorable person must say as Martin Luther said, "Here I stand; I can do no otherwise. God help me. Amen!"

5

Helpless, Hopeless, Fearful

One of the deepest valleys we are called to walk through is the feeling that something is wrong and there is nothing we can do about it. The book of Ecclesiastes begins with a mournful statement about the helplessness of people on this earth. That first chapter mournfully tells us that we work under the sun, but there is really no profit in it. One generation dies, and then another generation comes. But none of them really have any effect on the other. The sun rises, and the sun goes down, and there is nothing people can do about it. Likewise the wind blows around and around, but accomplishes nothing. The rivers run into the sea, but the sea never fills up. We are doomed here on an old earth ". . . and there is no new thing under the sun" (Ecclesiastes 1:9).

The New English Bible states it:

It is a sorry business that God has given men to busy themselves with. I have seen all the deeds that are done here under the sun; they are all emptiness and chasing the wind. What is crooked cannot become straight; what is not there cannot be counted.

Ecclesiastes 1:12–15

The author goes on to say, in the second chapter of Ecclesiastes, that he tried his hardest to make something out of life. He achieved position, gained wisdom, and did his best to make life a joyful experience; then he came to this conclusion, "I looked on all the works that my hands had wrought, and on the labour that I had laboured to do; and, behold, all was vanity and vexation of spirit, and there was no profit under the sun."

After a long struggle many people come to feel that life is controlled by nothing but fate. Nobody can tell what is going to happen next, and there seems to be no reward to us in trying to live a good life, because the good suffer just as much as the bad. A lot of people feel they might as well live it up, because they are going to die anyway, and in the end all our efforts are vain.

A sense of helplessness and hopelessness result in fearfulness. We are told over and over not to fear, because the Lord is with us and the Lord will take care of us. That's easy to say, but not as easy to live by. I like this story that I heard recently.

A mother was busy cooking supper in the kitchen and asked five-year-old Johnny to go into the pantry and get her a can of tomato soup. The little boy didn't want to go into the pantry alone, and he said, "Mommy, it's dark in there, and I'm scared." "It's all right, Johnny," she said. "You go in there and get a can of tomato soup. I need it for a recipe." He said, "But Mommy, it's dark, and I'm too scared to go in there by myself." "It's okay, Johnny," she said again. "Jesus will be in there with you. Now you go and get a can of tomato soup." Johnny went to the door and opened it slowly. When he peeked inside, it was dark, and he was scared. His hands began to tremble, but he got an idea. He said, "Jesus, if you're in there, would You hand me that can of tomato soup?" There are times when it is difficult to understand that "God is in there."

Illness is an experience that eventually comes to all of us. Nobody likes to be sick. It really isn't the sickness that upsets us; it is wondering whether or not we are going to get well. As long as we feel that a physician can do something, it is easy to have courage and faith. When we begin to feel that nothing can be done, then we become hopeless and fearful.

I recently spent an hour with a man who has given his life working in a big corporation. He told me of his dreams and his hopes when he started. He talked about how many days he would stay after the normal quitting time so he could get a little more in on his job. Then came that day when he was passed over, and another man was put in the place that he had sought. He felt all his efforts had been in vain. Helplessness immobilized this businessman, who wondered if he could continue to face life.

As long as we feel we can give our efforts and get results, we can have faith. But when we feel our best efforts get no results, we are in the depths of some valley.

It has been said that none of us want justice, we want mercy. Many times we feel helpless because we feel ashamed of what we have done and the way we have lived. We are afraid of what punishment might befall us.

I heard about a man who was being tried in court. The case was completed, and the jury withdrew to consider the verdict. The man had a very pressing engagement in another city, so he hurried from the courtroom to the airport, instructing his lawyer to send him a telegram as soon as the verdict was reached. When he registered in the hotel at his destination, the hotel clerk handed him a telegram. He knew it was from his lawyer, and he anxiously opened it. It contained only two words, *Justice prevailed.* Quickly he went to the telephone and sent a telegram back to his lawyer that said, *Appeal immediately.* One of our greatest fears is that we will get what we deserve. A feeling of unworthiness, of guilt, is a valley a lot of people are walking through. They never get away from the depths of the past.

The fear of the future is an even deeper valley for many people, who agonize about what might happen. Instead of facing it with fear, there is a much more wonderful way to look at the future. As children we anticipated what Santa Claus would bring us. As adults it is even more exciting to wonder what tomorrow will bring us. Not knowing the future is the most thrilling experience in life. Knowing the future takes all the fun out of living.

A few weeks before I wrote this, one of our local television stations taped a football game that was played in the afternoon and was to be shown immediately after the evening news. It was a game I was extremely interested in and was prepared to sit up and watch.

During the news broadcast, the announcer gave the score of the afternoon's game. Suddenly my interest began to wane, and before the first quarter was over, I had turned off the television and gone to bed. Who wants to watch a football game when you already know the final score?

Several years ago, I read this conversation in a delightful book entitled, *My Heart Shall Not Fear,* by Josephine Lott:

"Mother, if you could have foreseen what your married life was to be—would you have married dad?"

Nellie's blue eyes met her daughter's squarely. "Why, my dear, I'm afraid that if we could foresee what our lives would be, married or not, none of us would have had the courage to accept life. That's the reason we don't see the entire pattern—it isn't for us to see."

Rhoda sighed. "Well, I often think it would help in planning our lives, if we could see what's wrong. Why, Di and I were talking about it this morning. We would know at least what to avoid."

"If you girls think you would have avoided marriage, or married someone else, that's only another example of the misery a forecast of life might mean to you."

Nellie laughed as she stood up to remove the tray, "You'd be so cautious you'd be afraid to live at all." She patted Rhoda's thin cheek, rescued the slipping blanket from the side and floor, "You and Di and Jerry have the future, and that's all anyone should ask."

6

The Future You Have
Already Lived

More and more am I realizing that there is a great deal of satisfaction and joy in the future you have already lived. There was a time when my wife and I had three children at home. We felt deep responsibility for those children. We wanted to be with them, to care for them, to give them the best possible chance in life. One of the precautions we took for the benefit of our children was that we never flew in the same airplane, feeling that if one of us should be in an airplane crash the other one would be left to take care of the children. In those years, I never really felt comfortable on a plane. I worried about my responsibilities. Actually there was more danger in driving a car, especially the way I drove, but at least when I drove I felt in control. In an airplane I felt utterly dependent on somebody else, and in a sense I felt helpless.

Now, many years later, my circumstances are very different: My dear wife is in heaven; my children have their own homes and have established their places in life, which appear to be adequate. They love me as much as they ever did, but they do not depend on me as they once did.

Not long ago, I said to one of my sons that I have taken out a rather large accident-insurance policy. He replied, "If you were in an airplane that crashed, that insurance policy would not lessen our grief, but it surely would buy us a lot of handkerchiefs." Because they no longer depend on me in the same way, now my children and I laugh and joke with each other on this subject.

In my work I take about fifty plane trips a year. Several of those trips will be overseas. I now have learned to relax completely during the flight. There is no telephone ringing, nobody knocks on my door, and there really isn't much I can do, so I just lean back and either read or sleep and let the pilot take charge.

A lot of people deeply fear old age, but as I move in that direction, I think that is the most fearless time of life. You have already lived most of your future, so what do you have to worry about?

At this point six statements come to mind about the future:

1. People speak of "backing into the future." The future may be full of unknowns to us, but we have seen what is past.

2. The major events that determine the future have already happened and are irrevocable.

3. The best thing about the future is that it comes one day at a time.

4. I agree with the feelings of an editor about to be beheaded during the French Revolution. He said, "It is too bad to take off my head. I wanted to see how this thing was coming out."

5. The future is exciting; we are just in the beginning in every field of human endeavor.

6. When Saint Francis was asked what he would do if he knew he would die at sunset, he replied, "I would finish hoeing my garden." Today is still ours, with the obligation to live it to the fullest.

7

"When I Was Single My Pockets Would Jingle"

Many years ago I used to tease my wife by singing the old song:

> When I was single
> My pockets would jingle,
> I wish I was single again.

We would laugh together about that song, and usually she would make some comeback. A lot of people have laughed at that song, and then there comes a day when that song becomes very real and suddenly very serious. Being single and being single again are valleys that many people are called upon to walk through.

The Valley of the Single

Being single is a deliberate choice that many people make in our society today. There was a time when bachelors were accepted and even respected, but "old maids" were the objects of many cruel jokes and comments. Happily that day has passed.

The first time I ever became involved in politics was when I was a student in high school in Bowdon, Georgia. A young man who was running for the United States Senate came to our town. He was only twenty-nine years old at the time. I listened to him speak and was so impressed that afterwards I went up, shook hands with him, and told him I was going to work for him. That was the beginning of a personal friendship with Senator Richard B. Russell, of Georgia, which lasted until he died. He never told me why, but he did tell me that he chose never to get married. I never heard him criticized for that decision.

One of the things I have rejoiced in seeing our society develop is the opportunity for a woman to have a career. We honor and cherish motherhood, but we also hold in deep respect many women who have decided to devote their lives to their careers. For various reasons they have decided not to get married.

When one chooses the single life, it usually means that person has fulfilling experiences that compensate for the obvious sacrifices of being single. Despite loneliness, lack of intimacy with another person, the lack of the opportunity to share many deep thoughts and experiences, and so on, for these people the single life is not really a valley. It may be the freedom to achieve their greatest dreams and climb to extraordinary heights.

However there are many persons who have not chosen to be single. The fact is, some persons just have not been chosen, and they often feel left out of God's highest purposes in life.

In the Creation story we read, "It is not good that the man should be alone; I will make him an help meet for him" (Genesis 2:18). And Adam and Eve literally became a part of each other. Speaking of Eve, Adam beautifully said, " 'This is now bone of my bones, and flesh of my flesh. . . .' Therefore shall a man leave his father and his mother, and shall cleave unto his wife: and they shall be one flesh" (Genesis 2:23, 24). There is no more wonderful experience in all of life than the experience of being married.

Many, however, are not only denied that experience but suffer indignities because of it. I know a wonderful single person who is often asked, as most single people are, "Why have you not yet married?" And this person replies, "Because I have never found anybody who wanted me." This person usually says it with a smile on the face but with a tear in the heart. The fact of not being wanted by somebody is a cross many people are called upon to bear.

Bennett Cerf, who many remember as the master of ceremonies of the program "What's My Line?" was once asked, "What are you most afraid of?" His reply was, "I have to admit that the thing I am most afraid of is not being loved."

Many of us have laughed at Rodney Dangerfield's jokes about his not having respect, and most of us can identify with the first joke that he told. He said that as a little boy, in a game of hide and seek, he hid, but nobody came to seek him. To feel that nobody is seeking you, that nobody wants you, is one of the hardest crosses in life to bear.

Sometimes single people laugh and make jokes about themselves. Anthony Ewell wrote these words:

> As a beauty I am not a great star,
> There are others more handsome by far,
> But my face I don't mind it,
> For I am behind it,
> It's the people in front who get the jar.

We smile at such comments, but oftentimes the person who jokes about himself or herself really is not smiling. We can read all kinds of articles on how to improve ourselves and how to analyze our personalities, how to make friends with other people, and how to overcome our liabilities, and so on. But not being chosen as a life partner is a valley with shadows.

Here is the greatest appeal of the Christian faith. According to the Bible, Jesus never criticized a sinner. We need to learn that you do not win people through criticism, through condemnation, and through beating them over the head. Nobody is ever really changed by being told, "You are going to hell."

One of the ministers I admire the most is Dr. Walter Underwood. In one of his sermons he quotes Helmut Thielicke, who wrote:

> There is someone who knows you, someone who grieves when you go your own way, and it costs him something (namely the whole expenditure of life between the crib and the cross). But it costs him something to be the star to which you can look, the staff by which you can walk, the spring from which you can drink. If it is really true that there is someone who is interested in me and shares my life, then this can suddenly change everything, everything that I had hoped for and feared before.

To Be Single Again

Couples who have loved and lived together can be separated in several ways: death; divorce; illness that makes life together impossible; and perhaps the most cruel of all, living with someone under the same roof when that someone has ceased to care. Separation is truly a valley that is not easy to walk through.

Readjusting and starting over is very difficult. We find it hard to stand "at the grave of our hopes." Sometimes everything a person works for and longs for comes crashing down, and life literally falls apart. That person feels hostility and resentment toward others, toward life, and toward God. He feels guilt and self-condemnation. Many times he has no incentive to "get up and get going" again.

Let us recall a scene in the life of the great prophet Elijah. He was running for his life:

> But he himself went a day's journey into the wilderness, and came and sat down under a juniper tree: and he requested for himself that he might die; and said, It is enough; now, O Lord, take away my life; for I am not better than my fathers.
>
> 1 Kings 19:4

Many people have run away from life and sat down under a juniper tree, where they have sought to escape life. One of the songs by the Beatles proclaims, "I Believe in Yesterday." The juniper trees under which a lot of people are sitting are *yesterday*. These people keep looking back, sometimes longingly, sometimes with resentment, sometimes with a deep sense of guilt.

I heard, not long ago, of a church member who gave up going to football games. In explaining why he gave up watching the sport, the man gave four reasons:

1. At the last game he attended the persons sitting around him did not speak to him.
2. Every time he went to the game, the people in the ticket office were asking for money.
3. The band that played at halftime did not play the songs he liked.
4. Once he was sick and missed the game, and the coach did not call to find out what was wrong.

As painful as running away may be, it is a normal and natural experience. But forever sitting under a juniper tree is neurotic. That does not mean that adjusting to our new relationships will be easy.

It is not easy for a "single again" to return to normalcy, to overcome the disappointments, the sense of loneliness, and the hostilities. Sometimes the juniper tree is physical illness. Illness is one of the great escapes of life, and sometimes it is very real, born of shock, confusion, and depression. But you can't forever keep sitting under the juniper tree. I read about a shepherd who, one very cold morning, was leading his sheep out of the shelter of a valley and onto the plains. A passerby remarked that it seemed unwise to bring the sheep away from the protection of the valley. The shepherd carefully explained that snow would drift and pile high in the valley. If they stayed in what seemed a safe place, they would become trapped and doomed. Their only chance of safety was to go out into the open and face the storm.

During the past twenty-one years, I have been the minister of a church that now has more than 12,000 members. The other ministers on the staff and I conduct an average of four funerals every week. I am impressed by the way families who have buried loved ones are back in church the very next Sunday. Frequently when I stand in the pulpit to preach, I look into the faces of these people who have shown such courage and fortitude. Then I discover that instead of my preaching to them, they are preaching to me.

Taking the First Steps

As I have observed many people who are "single again," I have seen some of the causes that keep them successfully walking through the valley. When they find themselves alone, I find that many people do not panic; instead they take their time and make their decisions slowly. Just because a person is alone does not mean that he or she must sell the house tomorrow and move out.

Not long ago I was visiting a dear lady whose husband had died. She was showing me his favorite chair and told me that she had planned to move it out. But then she sat down in it one day and found it very comfortable, so she kept it. There are many things that we do not need to get rid of or even to change.

We love our children, and children are wonderful, but many times children are not as wise as their parents, even a single parent.

On one of my tours to the Holy Land, there was a lady who was ninety-two years old. She told me that her son and two daughters insisted she was too old to make that trip. She replied that it was her decision, and she intended to go. I really believe I have never seen a person enjoy a tour more, and she came home just bouncing with joy. In the valley of the shadow, one finds grief, but grief need not defeat anybody. In the midst of grief, many people discover their real selves, and as they fight to overcome boredom, self-pity, sorrow, and their negative emotions they gain a new strength and a new self-respect.

As they walk through grief many people learn to make their own decisions, to forget their old selves, and to begin being better and stronger persons. They realize the need to keep on living and loving.

There is marvelous power in accepting the fact that a change in our lives has occurred. Something has been lost, but new experiences can be found. The valley of the shadow of death is never a place to live; it is a place to go through.

In this respect one of the greatest inspirations to me was my mother. She was sixty years old when my father died. All her children were gone, and she was utterly alone. She said to me that her world had come to an end. She really felt there was no life left for her. But she lived twenty-seven years longer and, during those years, she had experiences she never dreamed of having. For example one of my sisters lived in Europe during the Second World War. As soon as the war was over, my mother went to New York to seek a way to go and see her daughter. Somehow she obtained passage on a freighter and spent three weeks at sea, but she landed on the coast of Europe. As she walked off the ship there was her daughter and three of her grandchildren to meet her. She lived a beautiful, full life during those twenty-seven years; and seeing her gave a lot of people—including me—inspiration to keep walking through the valley.

Life After Grief

We frequently hear the expression "life after death." In addition to this beautiful and wonderful hope, we have the opportunity of life after grief.

When we think of grief, so often we think of tragedies. But one of the most common grief situations in today's society is moving from one community to another. Family after family is uprooted. They are forced to leave their homes, their friends, and all their associations; it is not easy. The truth is, many people never really make it. In any city there are great numbers of people who have never made the transition.

There are many other grief situations, such as retirement, losing one's job, physical illness, financial reverses, and on and on they go.

One of the greatest hymns we have is "O Love That Wilt Not Let Me Go." It was written by Dr. George Matheson, one of the outstanding ministers in the Church of Scotland. His accomplishments were indeed impressive, and they become even more impressive when you learn that, at the age of fifteen, he became totally blind. It would have been so easy for him to surrender; instead he had a marvelous ministry. I especially like the third verse of that hymn:

> O Joy that seekest me thru pain,
> I cannot close my heart to Thee;
> I trace the rainbow thru the rain,
> And feel the promise is not vain
> That morn shall tearless be.

George Matheson wrote those words one day when he was alone in his house. His sister was married that day, and he felt both frightened and deserted. Truly he was writing out of a deep experience of grief. The fourth verse of that hymn goes like this:

> O Cross that liftest up my head,
> I dare not ask to fly from Thee;
> I lay in dust life's glory dead,
> And from the ground there blossoms red
> Life that shall endless be.

He was saying that life goes on. I love that last line, "Life that shall endless be."

One comic-strip character uses the expression, "Good grief," and truly grief can be good. Certainly there is life after grief, but many times there are changes. Yet frequently a sweet song comes out of grief.

There is a legend about a bird in Australia called the thornbird. The legend is that, from the moment many of these birds leave the nest, they go out in search of thorn trees and do not stop until the trees are found. Then they fly into the tree and pierce themselves upon thorns. As the birds die they sing out a song that is considered more beautiful than even that of the nightingale. Out of their agony comes their greatest song.

I have known people who are like the thornbird. They did not seek to be wounded on some thorn, yet being wounded, out of their agony came their sweetest songs.

Living Alone Though Living Together

I previously mentioned that in the church where I am the pastor, we have an average of four funerals a week. We also have an average of four weddings a week. I really feel that, next to the salvation of one's soul, marriage is the most important event in any person's life. A week or so after each wedding I write the couple a letter. In that letter, among other things, I say that one of the most important things about marriage, is to be accepted. I make a distinction between being loved and being accepted. Of course love is the basis of marriage, but there are many spouses who have never felt accepted. Marriage is not a reformatory, and couples need to reach out to each other without criticism or reservations. To live with a wife or a husband who does not accept one is a dark valley to walk through.

I like the words of William Hazlitt, "Man is the only animal that laughs and weeps; for he is the only animal that is struck with the difference between what things are, and what they ought to be."

Even in Grief the Unexpected May Happen

On one of my tours to the Holy Land, I said to our guide that I wanted to go to Emmaus. This is a place that tours do not usually go, because it is off the beaten track. But I am so glad that we drove those seven miles that day. For one thing, it brought to mind the story of those two people who were walking back to their home that

Sunday on which Jesus rose from the dead. They were sad, saying, "We trusted that it had been he which should have redeemed Israel . . ." (Luke 24:21). Their trust was in the past tense because they had seen Jesus die. He went into their house with them, and as He broke the bread they recognized Him, and they realized that He was alive again.

It was a wonderful experience for these sad people. Emmaus is a beautiful place. I really think one of the loveliest views in all Israel can be seen when one stands in Emmaus. It was at this place that Henry F. Lyte wrote that lovely song "Abide With Me." As our group stood there we talked about the experience of Emmaus and then we sang together those words:

> Abide with me—fast falls the eventide;
> The darkness deepens—Lord, with me abide;
> When other helpers fail and comforts flee,
> Help of the helpless, O abide with me!

There are times when all of us feel comfortless and helpless, but there is great strength in remembering the One who abides with us.

8

Through the Valley of "Why?"

"Yea, though I walk through the valley . . ." but the question is, "*Why?*" Whatever the valley may be, sooner or later each person who walks through it will ask the question "Why am I here?"

The first answer to that question is, we live in a law-abiding universe. Certain causes always produce certain effects.

Somewhere I read the story of a man who found himself wandering in Topsy-Turvy Land. It was an amazing story. He found people digging large holes in the ground, from which they would harvest their apples. He discovered that the trees had grown downward into the ground, instead of upward toward the sky. He poured himself a cup of tea from the teakettle on the stove. But as he took his first swallow of tea there was an agonizing pain in a sore tooth he had. The reason for the pain was that the water was freezing over the fire instead of boiling. The point is, in Topsy-Turvy Land one never knows what might happen: Trees might grow down instead of up, and water might freeze when heated instead of boiling.

Many years ago there lived an outstanding minister to whom people looked for guidance and inspiration. His wife developed a fatal illness. People wondered what he would say the Sunday after she died. Among other things he said, "The death of one whom we love is not too heavy a price to pay for an orderly and dependable universe."

Then we ask the questions: Is the universe hostile or friendly? Does God help us, or does God put our enemies here to hurt us? I like the story of the man who was being chased by a bear. He managed to catch hold of the limb of a tree and pull himself up just out of reach. And then he prayed, "O Lord, if you are not going to help me, for goodness sake, don't help that bear."

That reminds me of a little poem that Louie Edmondson, in Houston, wrote and sent to me:

A father was holding his son in his arms
A loud barking dog was near.
He knew his father would keep him from harm
And so he did not feel any fear.

When his father put him down
And set him upon a large log,
He gazed at his father from down on the ground
And said, "Please Father, now pick up the dog."

Time and again we say the same thing. We want God either to hold us in His arms and protect us from harm or else eliminate from the world that which could do us harm. We wonder why He does not do one or the other.

In my work as a minister, I have visited many patients in hospitals. Often I have asked a patient the question "Since you have been sick, what have people said to you?" And frequently I get one of three answers:

1. The patient is told that there is something in his or her life which is displeasing to God. "In some way you have broken God's law, and now, through this illness, God is telling you something."
2. Often patients have been told that illness is never God's plan or purpose. Illness is the work of Satan, therefore, the patient is told: "Build your faith. Keep believing and keep praying, and when your faith becomes strong enough, God will use it to overcome the evil of Satan."
3. Other people are told that they were selected by God to share in Christ's suffering; that suffering is a reward which shall be further rewarded; that God chooses people who are worthy, and He uses them as examples to increase the faith of other people. The idea is that some people have the privilege of being martyrs.

I do not believe any of these answers. As a very young minister I was called on to conduct the funeral for a very small child. After the service, a well-meaning but very ignorant woman said to the father,

"God is punishing you for the sins you have committed." I completely rebelled against that idea, and I have been rebelling ever since.

Illness is never God's will. When our oldest son was a little boy, there was an epidemic of polio in the community where we lived. One day we thought our son had some of the symptoms. We were frightened and prayed very earnestly that he be spared from polio. Fortunately we had misread his symptoms, but there were children who were not spared. However today God has answered that prayer for all children. Polio has never been God's will.

Recently I was talking to a physician who is a specialist in the area of children's needs. He told me that he could foresee the day when deafness would be eliminated from this earth; then there would be no more schools for deaf children. He showed me a tiny mechanism that can now be implanted in the brain of a person whose ears have no ability to hear. Through that mechanism, the brain picks up the sound. Deafness is not God's will; hearing is God's will. Through the skills of many wonderful people, God's will is being accomplished.

God never leads us into a valley to prove our faith. God gives us the faith to keep walking through the valley.

A father came to counsel with me about a great burden upon his heart. He had one son who was a student in college. He gave that boy a car. One day the boy was driving the car, had a wreck, and was killed. The father was grief stricken, and as he told me the story he kept saying, "If I had not given that boy a car, then he would not have had that wreck and would not have been killed." I kept saying over and over, "That is the risk you have to take."

You cannot keep your children locked up in their rooms and expect to save them from harm. Really to keep a child away from all of the possibilities of this life would be to utterly destroy that child. I cannot think of any worse pain than solitary confinement. God could have made a world where it would have been impossible for His children to become hurt, but it would also have been impossible for His children to grow and develop and to become like God, their Father.

Self-pitying martyrs never represent a God who created this earth.

Pain: Not God's Goof, God's Gift

Suppose you were to stick a pin in your finger and felt no pain. Immediately you would become very disturbed and seek medical help. The ability to feel pain is one of the most protecting gifts God has given us.

I like the phrase "the agony and the ecstasy." Actually, pain and pleasure are part and parcel of the same experience. The same nerve that carries the messages of pain to the human brain also carries the messages of pleasure. Over the same telephone wires you can send a loved one a message of joy or a message of sorrow. If someone does not want to hear the message of sorrow then the real solution is to cut the wire. But when you cut the wires, then communication is destroyed, and that is not what we want.

Earlier I stated that we all must feel some sorrow or pain. The worthwhile accomplishments of mankind are generally preceded by a long history of struggle. The pleasure is often not possible without the previous painful process.

Walk through a great museum such as the Louvre, in Paris, or the Sistine Chapel, in Rome. As you gaze upon the magnificent artistry of mankind, you need to remember the long, difficult hours that were spent in creating those masterpieces.

Perhaps the supreme example of pain that leads to joy is Jesus' example of childbirth. Nine months of waiting, of wondering, of anxiety, and then often, certainly in His day, excruciating pain. Childbirth has been thought of as agony, but then comes absolute ecstasy. Read again the words of Jesus:

> A woman when she is in travail hath sorrow, because her hour is come: but as soon as she is delivered of the child, she remembereth no more the anguish, for joy that a man is born into the world. And ye now therefore have sorrow: but I will see you again, and your heart shall rejoice, and your joy no man taketh from you.
>
> John 16:21, 22

Through the years I have loved these verses from one of John Greenleaf Whittier's beautiful poems.

The Eternal Goodness

I know not what the future hath
　Of marvel or surprise,
Assured alone that life and death
　His mercy underlies.

And if my heart and flesh are weak
　To bear an untried pain,
The bruisèd reed He will not break,
　But strengthen and sustain.

And so beside the Silent Sea
　I wait the muffled oar;
No harm from Him can come to me
　On ocean or on shore.

I know not where His islands lift
　Their fronded palms in air;
I only know I cannot drift
　Beyond His love and care.

That poem is very familiar, and we hear it quoted again and again. But John Greenleaf Whittier wrote another poem that we rarely hear quoted. Here is part of it:

Snow-Bound

Henceforward, listen as we will,
The voices of that hearth are still;
Look where we may, the wide earth o'er,
Those lighted faces smile no more. . . .
Yet Love will dream, and Faith will trust,
(Since He who knows our need is just,)
That somehow, somewhere, meet we must.
Alas for him who never sees
The stars shine through his cypress-trees!
Who, hopeless, lays his dead away,
Nor looks to see the breaking day
Across the mournful marbles play!
Who hath not learned, in hours of faith,

> The truth to flesh and sense unknown,
> That Life is ever lord of Death,
> And Love can never lose its own!

Our Freedom

One of the most cherished of all our blessings is what we call freedom: the freedom to choose, the freedom to act, the freedom to be. Without freedom, the saint and criminal would be on the same level. Without freedom, punishment for crime would be a total injustice. Without freedom, all religion would be meaningless.

Aldous Huxley once wrote that if a higher power would make him always do what was right, he would gladly accept the offer. But on the other hand, the very moment that he accepted the offer, he would cease to be a person and become a machine. He would have no decisions to make, no responsibilities to bear. God made man for good, but that must include the possibility of evil.

Dr. William Temple once wrote these words:

> A young man said, at last I have hit it—
> Since I cannot do right,
> I will find out tonight—
> The best sin to commit and commit it.

The fact is, we can do right; that is our fearful responsibility and also our crowning glory.

We often make a wrong assumption when we claim that the problem of evil and the problem of pain are synonymous. Many times evil and pain have no association with each other. A person can suffer without evil.

For many years a great professor at Yale University told the story of a soldier during the War Between the States, who was trying to get a mired cannon out of a deep ditch. A wandering preacher came by and saw it. He stood at the top of the ditch and called to the soldier below, "Are you saved, brother?" The soldier replied, "Don't ask me a bunch of silly questions; can't you see I am stuck in this ditch?"

Sooner or later every serious person who lives on this earth will identify with the cry of Jesus Christ from the Cross, "My God, my God, *why*—?" We blame God over and over when we do not understand. Many of us believe that *Hamlet* was the greatest play William Shakespeare wrote. In that play Ophelia, the sister of Laertes, was driven insane by cruelty. Laertes listened to her insane screaming; finally he could stand it no more and cried out, "Do you see this, O God?" Someone has shouted this defiance at God:

> That not for all thy power furled and unfurled,
> For all the temples to thy glory built
> Would I assume the ignominious guilt
> Of having made such men in such a world.

Though we cannot always answer the question "why?" we affirm the fact that we do not need to simply resign ourselves to living the rest of our lives in that valley. I heard a man once say, "If you can't have a piano on earth, you can have a harp in heaven." But my theory is, if you want a piano, you can keep working and at least try to get one. The idea of a harp in heaven does not take the place of a piano on earth. Heaven is not an opiate to deaden the pain that ought not to be. All suffering is not the result of sin, and neither is all suffering the will of God.

I am inclined to agree with the words of William Faulkner in his *Requiem for a Nun.* He said, "The salvation of the world is in man's suffering." Along the same line, Graham Greene, in *The Living Room,* said, "We always have to choose between suffering our own pain or suffering other people's. We can't not suffer."

"Yea, though I walk through the valley of the shadow of death . . ."—the point is, we do not sit down in despair, we do keep walking. I like the spirit of Justice Oliver Wendell Holmes, who once said, "If the good Lord should tell me I had only five minutes to live, I would say to Him, 'All right God, but I'm sorry you cannot make it ten.'"

I do not know the answer to "Why?" In fact the greatest interpreter of Christ and the Christian faith who ever lived did not know the answer either. That preacher was Paul, and I think the greatest sermon he ever preached—in fact the greatest sermon that has ever been preached on this earth (other than the Sermon on the Mount)—is contained in the fifteenth chapter of 1 Corinthians. He concludes that glorious statement of the Christian faith with these wonderful words:

> Behold, I shew you a mystery; We shall not all sleep, but we shall all be changed, In a moment, in the twinkling of an eye, at the last trump: for the trumpet shall sound, and the dead shall be raised incorruptible, and we shall be changed. For this corruptible must put on incorruption, and this mortal must put on immortality. So when this corruptible shall have put on incorruption, and this mortal shall have put on immortality, then shall be brought to pass the saying that is written, Death is swallowed up in victory. O death, where is thy sting? O grave, where is thy victory? The sting of death is sin; and the strength of sin is the law. But thanks be to God, which giveth us the victory through our Lord Jesus Christ.

Those are glorious words, but those words are not the end of Paul's sermon. He has one thing more to say. Lest we should surrender to the fact that the only answer to "Why?" is in eternity, St. Paul goes on to say, "Therefore, my beloved brethren, be ye stedfast, unmoveable, always abounding in the work of the Lord, forasmuch as ye know that your labour is not in vain in the Lord." That is, no matter what the "Why?" might be, we know that steadfast faithfulness on this earth is not in vain.

"There Will Be Peace in the Valley"

9

Valley Thoughts

One of the songs that I really like the best—especially when Tennessee Ernie Ford sings it—goes like this:

> I am tired and weary but I must toil on
> Till the Lord comes to call me away,
> Where the morning is bright and the lamb is
>   the light
> And the night is as fair as the day.
>
> There'll be Peace In The Valley for me some day,
> There'll be Peace In The Valley for me.
> I pray no more sorrow and sadness or trouble
>   will be,
> There'll be Peace In The Valley for me.

"Peace in the valley"—really that says it all. In the Twenty-third Psalm David said, "Yea, though I walk through the valley . . ." but if there is peace in the valley, so what? We do not mind the valley if somehow we can make peace with it.

When we find ourselves in the valley, there are many thoughts that come to mind. We want security and are constantly afraid of what might happen tomorrow. We want to control our own lives, but we know that we are subject to many circumstances that we cannot control. At times we do not want to face up to the life we live or the persons we are, and we seek to escape. We look back through the years and we think about rewards we worked for but that somehow never materialized. There were times when we wanted revenge for being mistreated or being left out. There are other times when it just seemed as if existence was dull and drab and not worth the effort. We have felt abandoned, isolated, forgotten. We have been criticized, and criticism hurts.

As we have found ourselves in some valley, we have felt rejection, and that is hard to bear. We look back and remember how hard we worked for material gain; then we realize how little satisfaction it brought when we got it. Sometimes in the very midst of success, we feel a sense of failure. We have felt that we were in the midst of a lot of people, yet we did not feel related to anybody. Many times we wanted to talk, to express our feelings, to reveal our hurts and our problems, but there was nobody to listen who would understand. Sometimes we have wondered why God allows any more babies to be born in such a world when we see where it is heading. We have felt there is no real direction or meaning or significance to life. Sometimes we reach the point of feeling that even though there is a future, we are not sure that we want it, because we do not know what that future might be. "Down in the valley" sometimes we are inclined to say, "Is there anything that really matters anymore?"

10

Make Your Worries Behave

One summer night I went to another state to speak to a large gathering of young people. They were meeting in a mountainous area in a camp. Most of them were teenagers, and it was a thrilling experience being with them. I listened to a song several were singing as they walked by the cabin in which I was staying. The verse I heard went like this:

> Always in the moonlight,
> I want to hold somebody's hand.
> Always in the moonlight,
> I seem to understand.
> Why all the little beeses and all the little bearses
> Never go in threeses, always go in pairses.

Hearing that song and seeing their faces almost made me want to be sixteen years old again. There in the mountains, as I sat waiting for suppertime and my speech, which was to follow, I looked up and suddenly the majestic words of a Psalm came to mind. Psalm 95 begins talking about singing unto the Lord and making a joyful noise. It talks about the greatness of God and then you read these words: "In his hand are the deep places of the earth: the strength of the hills is his also" (Psalms 95:4). Sitting in those lovely mountains, the words of the Psalmist had real meaning. Maybe I am in a valley, but the valley is in God's hands. All around me are great mountains, and they are strong and have been there a long time. They represent the strength of Almighty God. Even though you are sitting in a valley, when you begin looking at those big, powerful mountains, your worries begin to pale.

We need to remember that the very existence of a problem is proof that there is a solution. The reason I say this is because the entire world is based on a system of opposites: good and evil, white and black, high and low, night and day, love and hate, light and dark, long and short, pain and pleasure, sickness and health, and on and on they go. When you know there is a solution, a lot of the worry goes out of any situation.

11

Twenty-four Steps to Peace in the Valley

How can you find peace in the valleys of your life? Here are some excellent steps everyone can take to discover that way of life.

1. Begin with the fact that worry is a habit. Just like any other habit, it can be faced, dealt with, and overcome. Often we do not worry about specific trouble; rather we worry because we have acquired a bad habit.

2. When you are upset, put skid chains on your tongue. Most of us have a tendency to talk too much when we are disturbed. We need to think more and say less, rather than say more and think less.

3. Practice the art of a cheerful countenance. Sometimes it is better to smile than it is to cry. To hide your pains and worries and disappointments under a smile can oftentimes lead to a cheerful heart.

4. Go ahead and cry. This is not contradictory to the idea of being cheerful. There are times when we need to cry, and sometimes our tears will bathe our souls. There are times to hide our emotions and times to express our emotions. We need to be able to know the difference.

5. Believe that inner turmoil and tension and frustrations can really harm your life. Inner disturbances can disintegrate one's soul. It is not good to be upset inside. Peace is a lot healthier than war.

6. When you are disturbed and bothered, analyze your problems. It has been said that 40 percent of the things that disturb us are in the past; 50 percent of the things we worry about are in the future; only 10 percent of the things we worry about are problems we can deal with today. Separate your upsetting thoughts and deal with that 10 percent you can deal with now.

7. When something in the past is worrying you, decide whether or not you can do anything about it. If there is something you cannot change, then settle it with God and trust His forgiving mercy. If it is

something you can do something about, then do it. Maybe it means making an apology; maybe you should see to the payment of a debt. On the other hand, don't ruin your life today because of the impossibility of doing anything about yesterday. Recently I had a long talk with a man who is destroying his life because he spoke unkindly to his mother. Now she is dead, and he can do nothing about it. It is stupid to destroy yourself utterly and needlessly.

8. Practice forgetting. I say *practice* because it is not easy, and actually no person ever completely forgets. Paul tells us, ". . . this one thing I do, forgetting those things which are behind, and reaching forth unto those things which are before" (Philippians 3:13). He never would have been such a great preacher if he had somehow not learned the art of forgetting.

9. When you are disturbed and churning inside, make promises very sparingly. Sometimes under strain and stress we promise a lot more than we need to or ought to. Most promises should be made in a spirit of calmness and peace.

10. When you are walking through the valley, keep an open mind on the debatable questions. That is, plan to talk calmly, to think but not to argue. To disagree is not bad, but under the strain and stress that many people feel, disagreement can lead to permanent damage. Oftentimes the settlement of an argument can lead to peace; but more often, efforts to settle an argument under strain and stress lead to disaster.

11. When we are upset, we are tempted to talk about the vices of other people. But this is a time to say nothing, unless we can say something good. Time and again people have made comments they wish they had never made. There are times when saying nothing is the very best course.

12. Sometimes people say unpleasant things about us. In fact this is one of the greatest reasons people get upset and disturbed. I do not say that we should pay no attention to the remarks of others. There are times when we should consider those statements and ask ourselves if they are justified. If these comments are not valid, there are times when the person who made those remarks should be faced with them. However the time to deal with these unhappy remarks about ourselves is not while we are in the valley.

13. The wisest psychologist America has ever produced was Wil-

liam James. He once said, "The essence of genius is to know what to overlook." There are some things that are just not worth bothering about.

14. Many times we are too self-centered and to develop interest in other people—in what they are doing, in their need, in their joys and sorrows—brings to us great rewards. We need to develop the habit of making everyone we meet, however humble that person may be, feel that he or she is important.

15. Never tell a joke at somebody else's expense. One of my heroes was Jack Benny. I listened to him again and again. He made the world laugh, but if you remember, he made the world laugh at himself. He never belittled somebody else to get a joke.

16. Stop worrying about whether or not you have been duly rewarded. Do your work, be patient, keep a cheerful disposition, and you can be certain that eventually you will receive the respect due you. Don't worry about it; you will be recognized. Believing that, you are under less strain.

17. One of the greatest words to learn is *imperturbability.* That means that no matter what happens, you are going to be calm and peaceful. You are not going to let outside events destroy you inside.

18. Remember that today is not the last day that you are going to live. There is also a tomorrow, and you do not have to get everything done and everything settled today. Affirm your faith in the future.

19. At night when you come in from a day's work, before you sit down to dinner, you go and wash your hands. It is also a marvelous experience to practice washing out of our minds the unhappy thoughts and experiences of that day. It is marvelous to empty your minds of any insecurity you may feel.

20. Every so often, you need to stop by a filling station and fill up the gasoline tank of your automobile. Otherwise your automobile will stop running. So it is with the human mind; we need to practice filling our minds with those positive thoughts that lead to courage and calmness and joy. Too many of us find ourselves in a valley because we did not stop to fill up our minds.

21. Do not waste your worries. On the other hand let your worries become the stimulus for positive action. The ability to worry is a gift of God. You are created that way, and God gave us this ability for a

purpose. One of the main purposes of worry is to make us get up and get going in some positive way. If you are in the valley, do something. God said to the prophet Isaiah, ". . . in quietness and in confidence shall be your strength" (Isaiah 30:15). However in that same chapter are these words, "And thine ears shall hear a word behind thee, saying, This is the way, walk ye in it" (Isaiah 30:21). There are times when we do need to be still and quiet, and in those moments we gain strength. But strength is to be used in action. Wasted strength is a tragedy.

22. Change your concerns from being self-centered and make them other centered. Somebody spoke these words:

> Lord, lay some soul upon my heart,
> And love that soul through me;
> And may I bravely do my part
> To win that soul for Thee.

When we become outreaching in our attitudes and in our actions, marvelous blessings return unto us. Read again and again the words of Jesus when He said, "He that findeth his life shall lose it: and he that loseth his life for my sake shall find it" (Matthew 10:39). Again and again people have found peace in the valley by becoming absorbed in the needs of someone else.

23. Develop the art of praise, instead of criticism. Oftentimes when we correct somebody, we try to make ourselves believe that we are interested in helping that person. But most of the people who pick out flaws in other people are expressing their own insecurity. Start praising other people, and you will find your own inner problems diminishing.

24. Let every inner disturbance be a call to exercise your own faith. Remind yourself of your need for God and an assurance of God's presence. The great poet Edwin Markham said it like this:

> He walked as one who has done with fear,
> Knowing at last that God is near.

One of the most familiar of all the hymns says it as well as it can be said, but sometimes familiarity obscures meanings. Think about the hymn, "What a Friend We Have In Jesus" and meditate upon these words from that hymn:

> O what peace we often forfeit,
> O what needless pain we bear,
> All because we do not carry,
> Ev'rything to God in prayer.

Nels Ferre was a wonderful scholar. He wrote some marvelous books, and in one of those books he tells about a dream his wife had. She was sitting at a table. She had been given the task of writing down on a sheet of paper the answer to the question "How can I quit worrying?" In her dream she wrote at great length, but when she woke up, she could remember only the three words of her outline; they were: *worship, work,* and *wait.* If one cannot remember these twenty-four steps, I really think that peace can be brought to the valley with those three key words: worship, work, and wait.

One of the greatest ministers America has ever produced was Phillips Brooks. Several times when I have been in Boston, I have stood at the front of Trinity Church and looked at the statue of that great preacher who preached there for so many years. Whenever I visit Bethlehem, I always think of the song he wrote:

> O little town of Bethlehem,
> How still we see thee lie!
> Above thy deep and dreamless sleep
> The silent stars go by.

It is one of the most beautiful of all the Christmas carols. Once Phillips Brooks said that one of the most important lessons he ever learned was when he was a young boy. He was at the family dinner table. Times were hard, and the Brooks household was having difficulties. His mother, in a moment in despair, spoke bitterly about the injustice of it all. When she had finished, he remembered that his father said quietly, "I have trusted the Lord for forty years, and I do not mean to stop now."

When you take all of your troubles and face up to them in the most practical and reasonable way, you truly can find peace in the valley.

12

"God Don't Sponsor No Flops"

Ethel Waters said, "God don't sponsor no flops," and that is the truth.

Whenever I visit the Holy Land, I am always amazed and astonished all over again. I live in the United States, a large land with great natural resources, the most powerful nation on earth. In this land we have great industry, magnificent universities, the most advanced research, and we Americans are quite proud of ourselves.

Compared to our nation, Israel is small. Golda Meir once said that Moses wandered for forty years and settled in the only place in the Far East where there is no oil. Really there is only a little oil in Israel and very few natural resources. Much of the land is arid and hilly and unusable. It's a small, weak country. You wonder why God chose Israel.

I will never forget that one of the members on one of our tours expressed the very thoughts I have written above. But just as we were beginning to leave, he came to me and said, "You know there is something about this country that gets ahold of you, I can't describe it, but I don't want to leave."

In fact many of the people who have been on our Holy Land tours have later gone with us a second time. I know the feeling that man described. I have been to Israel twenty times, yet I get more excited about each trip I go on. I can't describe it, but it gets ahold of me.

Then I think about Jesus. God sent His Son to be the Saviour of the world. He chose that little girl who lived in Nazareth to be the mother. She wasn't the daughter of some powerful king; she had no great wealth or even education. The schools there were extremely limited. Nazareth was so small that all the people in the town could get their water from one well. You can stop and drink from that same well today.

There was Jesus. He never went to a university. In just a few hours in a jet airplane, one can travel more miles than He traveled in His entire lifetime. He was a very obscure person until He was thirty years old; He died when He was thirty-three. That was Jesus. You wonder about the persons Jesus chose to be His followers. We talk about the Sea of Galilee. It is a beautiful, wonderful place, but it is not much more than a big lake. The most outstanding disciple He had, in my opinion, was Simon Peter. Simon Peter had spent his working life fishing that little body of water. He wasn't important; he didn't know anybody important; and yet Jesus took him.

When you think of Israel, of Mary, of Jesus, and of Simon Peter, you just know "God don't sponsor no flops."

This is very encouraging. So many people feel insignificant, unworthy, and unimportant. The truth of the matter is, there are no unimportant people and no unimportant events. A man sat in the shade of a tree and saw an apple fall and discovered the law of gravity. His name was Isaac Newton. Another man sat in the kitchen and saw a teakettle steam. It was a significant experience because, seeing that teakettle, he discovered the principle of the steam engine. His name was Robert Fulton. There are no insignificant people or insignificant events. Everything in God's creation is important.

Somewhere I read the story of a Boston landlady who was interviewing a prospective tenant. In order to impress her, he took his wallet out of his pocket and showed her its contents. She replied, "Do not show me your wallet, show me your beliefs." She is completely right. The most important thing about a person is not how much money that person has or how many honors that person received; the most important element is what a person believes. I could not count the times, during my life, when I have reminded myself of that little train that puffed its way up a hill, saying, "I think I can, I think I can, I think I can." Eventually it made it up the hill.

Isaac Watts wrote one of the great hymns of the church, "Alas! And Did My Savior Bleed?" The last line of the first verse of that hymn says, "Would he devote that sacred head For such a worm as I." Many years ago, I decided I would never sing those words. I may be a worm, but I am not going to sing about it. The truth is, I do not believe I am a worm, so it pleased me greatly when the hymnal of my own church was revised and the word *worm* was changed to *sinner*. I know I am a sinner, but I am not a worm.

No person is here by accident; every person is a child of God. The writer of the book of Genesis says that when God created the earth and all of the creatures of the earth, including man, "God saw every thing that he had made, and, behold, it was very good . . ." (Genesis 1:31).

Whoever I may be, let me assure myself that my value as a person is not determined by how much money I have accumulated, what honors I have received, or what goals I have achieved; my value is in just being me.

I have a close minister friend who one day said this, "My parents felt the pressure to succeed. I felt that they loved me, but when I achieved something special, they really poured on more love. I came to believe that the love of my parents for me was in ratio to what I accomplished as a person." Then he went on to say, "I wonder if this is not one of the real problems in our society. Children and young people are getting pressure from their parents to excel. This same pressure operates in our schools, our social climate, and every area of life. No wonder many people give up in hopeless despair."

One reason we find ourselves in "the valley of the shadow of death" is because we have not lived up to what somebody else thought we should be or do. Thus, feeling belittled, we have lost confidence in ourselves, and we feel unworthy and defeated.

Ethel Waters was right, "God don't sponsor no flops."

I get inspiration from that line in the play *Green Pastures* when Noah says to the Lord, "I ain't very much, but I'se all I got." We can all say the same thing.

13

Stop, Look, Listen

At railroad crossings we see the familiar sign that tells us STOP, LOOK, LISTEN. Obedience to that sign will prevent motorists from having accidents with the trains. This is not a bad sign to occasionally obey in the journey of life.

I have been greatly blessed by the writings of Arthur Gordon. Some time ago he wrote a book entitled *A Touch of Wonder*. In that book he tells about being in a valley. It was one of those bleak periods when it seems everything is stale and flat; his energy and enthusiasm were gone, and his days seemed barren. Finally in desperation, he went to a doctor. Happily the doctor was a very wise practising physician. After examining him and finding nothing wrong physically, this doctor asked him the question, "Where were you happiest as a child?"

Arthur Gordon replied, "Why, at the beach, I suppose. We had a summer cottage there. We all loved it."

The doctor told him to go to the beach the following morning and arrive not later than nine o'clock. He was not to take anything to read, nothing to write on, and no radio to listen to. He gave him four prescriptions and told him, "Take these at nine, twelve, three and six o'clock."

The next day Arthur Gordon went to the beach as he had been directed. When he got there at nine o'clock, he opened the first prescription. It read, LISTEN CAREFULLY.

He described how he sat there for three hours and listened to the sounds: the roar of the sea, the cry of the birds, the wind, and all the other sounds. He began to think of the great immensity of the life about him. He realized that he was not the biggest thing in the universe, and he remembered a phrase from Carlyle, "Silence is the element in which great things fashion themselves."

At twelve o'clock he opened the second prescription, and it said,

TRY REACHING BACK. He began to think back over the experiences of his life, the ones that had meant something to him.

At three o'clock he opened the third prescription, which read, RE-EXAMINE YOUR MOTIVES. At first he felt defensive, but then he saw that "if one's motives are wrong, nothing can be right."

Finally, at six o'clock he opened the fourth prescription, which simply said, WRITE YOUR WORRIES IN THE SAND. He tells how he wrote several words in the sand, and then he says, "Then I walked away, and I did not look back. I had written my troubles on the sand. The tide was coming in."

I think that is one of the most marvelous experiences I have ever read about. And it is an experience that any one of us can have if we will just do it. We do not need to go to the beach, but we do need to be willing to take off some time and do it.

Listen, Rest

A few weeks ago I felt tired. I wasn't sick, I was just tired. So I made up my mind that I was going to spend the next day in bed. I decided I would get up in the morning, eat a light breakfast, and go back to bed. Then at noon I would eat a light lunch and go back to bed. Finally at dinner I would eat something and go back to bed. I would not listen to the radio or the television. If I slept, that was good. If I didn't sleep, that was also good. I purposed to spend just one entire day resting in bed. I did it, and it was a marvelous experience. I felt better for weeks after that, and by taking off a day to rest, I got much more accomplished later on.

You might not take an entire day, but sometimes it is a marvelous experience to take some time to stop and think about the world in which you live and your part in it. In the story of creation, as recorded in the first chapter of the Bible, we learn that, stage by stage, as He created the earth, "God saw that it was good." It does something to any one of us when we are depressed and unhappy to stop long enough to think about the fact that we live in a good world, a world that provides a shelter and clothing and food and opportunities and so much more. Here is a world that has a sun to shine over it by day and a moon by night, a world that has fertile fields and flowing rivers, and wide oceans. Our world is surrounded by a blanket of air, so man can breathe; it contains people, and a lot of them are good.

However as we think of all the good things of the world, sometimes it does us good to realize that God not only made the world, but that He made the laws by which the world must be governed. These laws insure the permanency of the world. There is the law of gravitation, the law of seasons, the law of the rotation of the earth around the sun, and many other physical laws without which it would be impossible to live on this earth.

Not only that, as we stop and listen to the world, we also remember that God made the laws by which people live on this earth. He did not make those laws to restrict us, but to give us life. If we are pressed and unhappy and feel that we are living in the valley, it just might be that we have broken some of God's laws for our lives. In so doing we have hurt ourselves, and now we are suffering because of our disobedience. As we stop and listen we gain respect for the orderly processes of living. We begin to get our thinking straightened out.

Remember

The next step we need to take is to remember. What a blessed and wonderful thing a memory is! My brother, John, was only fifteen months younger than I. We literally grew up together. We slept together, we played together, and we shared all our possessions. Neither of us ever talked about "my baseball" or "my skates" or even "my money." We were real brothers in the truest sense of the word.

As little children we learned to kneel and pray together at the bedside every night. We prayed that simple little prayer, "Now I lay me down to sleep...."

Long after both of us became men, we took an automobile trip together, just the two of us. We were gone for about two weeks. I never shall forget the first night, when we started to bed. We had not slept in the same room for more than twenty-five years. But that night as we started to bed we both just naturally knelt and prayed our prayer. It did not seem unusual or strange in any way.

Then one night, about twelve o'clock, my phone rang, and it was Sue, John's lovely wife. She said to me, "Charles, John had a heart attack, and he died." The first thing that came to my mind was that prayer we prayed together, which goes on to say, "If I should die before I wake, I pray Thee, Lord, my soul to take." I loved John; and I suppose, up to that moment in my life, the word that John had died was about the lowest point I had ever experienced. Truly I was in the valley. Remembering that shared prayer gave me marvelous assurance.

Memory is a blessed, wonderful experience. One of the preachers I have loved through the years is Dr. Ralph W. Sockman. He was my personal friend and a great inspiration. I have all of his books. Now there comes to my mind a passage from one of them, *The Higher Happiness,* in which he tells the following story:

> According to an ancient Greek legend, a woman came down to the River Styx to be ferried across to the Region of Departed Spirits. Charon, the kindly ferryman, reminded her that it was her privilege to drink the waters of Lethe, and thus forget the life she was leaving. Eagerly she said, "I will forget how I suffered." And, added Charon, "Remember too, that you will forget how you have rejoiced." The woman said, "I will forget my failures." The old ferryman added, "And, also, your victories." She continued, "I will forget how I have been hated." "And also how you have been loved," added Charon. Then she paused to consider the whole matter, and the end of the story is that she left the draught of Lethe untasted, preferring to retain the memory even of sorrow and failure, rather than give up memory of life's loves and joys.

Some time to stop and remember will do more to keep us going through the valley than anything else.

God has given to mankind two wonderful lights. One is the light of hope, which pierces into the darkness of the future and bids us keep going. The other is the light of memory, which takes us by the hand and leads us back through the happy scenes and experiences of yesterday. In the light of memory, we see scenes that inspire us and give us strength to weather living; we realize that the hurts and tragedies of life can be overcome. To be quiet and still and listen to the world about us and to let our minds reach back into yesterday is a marvelous experience.

Our Motives

Third, sometimes it is great for our souls to stop and examine our motives. After all, why are we living? There is a book entitled, *Making It,* by Norman Podhoretz. In the preface of that book he writes:

> Let me introduce myself. I am a man who at the precious age of thirty-five experienced an astonishing revelation; it is better to be a success than a failure. Having been penetrated by this great truth concerning the nature of things, my mind was now open the first time to a series of corollary perceptions, each one as dizzying in its impact as the Original Revelation itself. Money, I now saw (no one, of course, had ever seen it before), was important; it was better to be rich than poor. Power, I now saw (moving on to higher subtleties) was desirable; it was better to give orders than to take them. Fame, I now saw (how courageous of me not to flinch) was unqualifiedly delicious; it was better to be recognized than to be anonymous.

He goes on in that book to say many good and worthwhile things, but in the very preface he is lifting up the fact that many people very quickly measure life by four words: *success, money, power,* and *fame.*

It was Vince Lombardi who was truly a great football coach, who said, "Winning isn't everything; winning is the only thing." Along that same line, Leo Durocher, a famous baseball legend said, "Nice guys finish last."

What are our motives? What are we really seeking in life? What do we feel makes us successful?

I really believe that the major influence on my idea of success was my father's life. I grew up as a little boy feeling that my father was the greatest man in the world. Through all the years, I have never had occasion to change that opinion. Yet according to the world's idea of "making it," my father would not have been considered a success. He was a preacher, but he never served very large churches. In fact, when I was twenty-seven years old, I was appointed to a church that was larger than any my father ever served in during his life. When he died, he had $200 in the bank, and that was all. Having the picture of him before me across these years has greatly influenced my thinking about life. I am not nearly as impressed with the so-called standards of success set by the world as I would have been had it not been for my own father.

Several years ago I went to preach at the homecoming service of a little church in the mountains of North Georgia. When I finished seminary, I had been appointed to four little mountain churches. On the way to the church that Sunday morning when I was to preach, I stopped along the side of the road and turned off the car's motor. There was a big pile of sawdust, but I remembered when there was a sawmill there. I remembered that the pavement on the road ended at that place; and the distance from there to the little church, about two miles away, was connected by a very narrow dirt road. In the wintertime ice and snow often made it impossible to drive from the sawmill to the church, so I would park at the sawmill and walk to the church. When I got there, I would get some wood out from under the building, make a fire, and sweep up around the stove. Eventually ten or fifteen people would come, and I would preach to them. One Sunday a month, for three years, I went to that church. They paid me fifty dollars a year, a little more than four dollars per month.

As I sat by the side of that sawmill site, I kept asking myself two questions, "Why did I go?" and "Would I go again?" I could sincerely say that I went because I believed in what I was doing, and if circumstances were such, I would do it again today. I have never worked for the rewards. I am happy to have the rewards I have received, but I am just as sure I would have acted in the same fashion without them.

Success

We need to remind ourselves that whatever we call success is really a pathway and not a final destination. Success is never the goal in life, but the way to reach the goal we have set for ourselves. Success is the opportunity to express our abilities fully, and what is success for one person may not at all be success for another. We need to take personal success out of the arena where we judge ourselves by other people's lives and by what other people think.

There is a vast difference between success and self-destructive striving. Examine your life and ask yourself questions such as this one: Do you always feel in a hurry? There are a lot of people who feel they never have time for many of the things in life they want. They are reluctant to go on a vacation, to take an afternoon off to go fishing, or to play a game of golf.

Concerning our expectations for success, Albert Ellis, a psychotherapist, gave twelve wonderful facts:

1. It is unrealistic to believe that everyone is going to agree with us all the time, like us all the time, love us all the time. We should not expect it.

2. It is unrealistic to believe that we can be successful in every venture, that we can be perfect in all we attempt to do or be. No one ever has been, no one ever will be.

3. It is unrealistic to believe that there is any job, almost any task, that doesn't have its frustrations, its discouragements, its disappointments. Some have more than others, but they are always there.

4. It is unrealistic to believe there is any relationship in home, work, or play that doesn't have some tensions, some stress, some differences. As long as we deal with people, we will deal with problems.

5. It is unrealistic to believe there is any place, city, church, or neighborhood, that is ideal, is completely free from problems, or does not need change or improvement. There is no such thing as Utopia.

6. It is unrealistic to believe that we will ever be completely free from feelings of guilt, doubt, inadequacy, anxiety, or anger. They are part of being human. They need to be understood and controlled, but they are always present.

7. It is unrealistic to feel that others should be blamed for all they say and do. All people have their own problems and ten-

sions. Most people want to do better. If we understood people's backgrounds, we would probably understand their behavior.

8. It is unrealistic to feel we are entirely victims of fate or outside circumstances, that we have no control over what we think, feel, or do.

9. It is unrealistic to avoid life, to refuse to face life honestly.

10. It is unrealistic to feel that we are the way we are, that we are conditioned by past experiences or environmental circumstances and therefore cannot change.

11. It is unrealistic to believe we can quickly achieve anything significant or that we can change in a hurry. Achievement and change are possible, but they usually come slowly and in small steps.

12. It is unrealistic to feel that there is only one solution to any given situation or that things are catastrophic if we do not find a solution.

Let the Past Be the Past

The final prescription that wise and wonderful physician gave to Arthur Gordon was: WRITE YOUR WORRIES IN THE SAND.

There come times when some things should be done with. I mention my father often. The last six weeks of his life he was in a hospital, and much of the time he did not have his mental faculties. I would sit with him by the hour during those weeks; one day he opened his eyes and looked at me and said, "Charles, do you know the greatest word in the English language?" My reply was, "Papa, what would you say it is?" As long as I live I shall never forget his reply. He said, "The greatest word is *forgiveness.*" Then he went back to sleep. After a while I got up and drove about thirty miles, from the hospital to my home. Just as I walked into the house, my phone rang; a nurse from the hospital was calling to say that my father had died. I have reason to believe that the last word he ever spoke was *forgiveness.* I find great inspiration and joy in remembering that.

Through the years I have talked with many people who were emotionally upset. I have discovered that we have many kinds of problems in life and that learning to be bigger than our problems is one of life's greatest experiences. It is not easy to maintain self-respect in the face of devastating experiences. It is not easy to keep looking forward when we have made big mistakes or done something we know is wrong.

We do all need to remember, however, that there are some things we can do nothing about. There are some things we need to write in the sand and walk away from, letting the tide wash them away.

Someone tells of a school teacher who brought a quart bottle of milk to school one morning and set it on her desk. Later in the day she announced that she intended to teach the class one of life's most important lessons. Then she took that bottle of milk and hit it against the side of the desk, breaking the bottle into many pieces. The milk spilled all over the floor.

The teacher asked the class to examine the wreckage. She explained that it was impossible to put that bottle back together again, and certainly it was impossible to gather up all that milk and put it back in the bottle. "Therefore," she went on to explain. "When something happens that you cannot help or do anything about, always remember this one lesson: Don't cry over spilled milk."

I remember the words of Omar Khayyam:

> The Moving Finger writes; and having writ,
> Moves on: nor all your Piety nor Wit
>   Shall lure it back to cancel half a Line
> Nor all your Tears wash out a Word of it.

There are times when we need to go back and change things, but there are also times when we need to write them in the sand, letting the waves of God's mercy wash over those words and forever eradicate them. Reinhold Niebuhr said it best, in *The Irony of American History:*

> Nothing that is worth doing can be achieved in our lifetime; therefore we must be saved by hope. Nothing which is true or beautiful or good makes complete sense in any immediate context of history; therefore we must be saved by faith. Nothing we do, however virtuous can be accomplished alone; therefore we are saved by love. No virtuous act is quite as virtuous from the standpoint of our friend or foe as

it is from our standpoint. Therefore we must be saved by the final form of love which is forgiveness.

Ought, Want, Do

When we are in some valley of life, there are three feelings that we have: the feeling of what we *ought* to do, the feeling of what we *want* to do, and the feeling of what we *actually* do. There is marvelous power in human life when those three feelings get together. When what we ought, what we want, and what we actually do become one, the walls of the valley seem to melt away, and we stand on higher ground.

1. The first temptation is to leave out and ignore *ought*. There are many people who feel life should be controlled by our wants and our impulses, and that is the pathway to peace. We went through a period called the New Morality. The trouble was that it was neither new nor moral—in fact, it was the oldest downfall of mankind. Go back in history and over and over we find people who worshiped their desires. Bacchus was the Greek god of appetite, and for many people he still is their supreme god. But Bacchus never ultimately saves anybody.

There are certain *oughts* in life, and to ignore them is to eventually end up in the lowest of all valleys. We do some things, we live our lives certain ways because we know what we ought to do.

2. There are other people who seek to solve all their problems by getting rid of the *wants* of life. They preach to themselves that they should live strictly by the *oughts* and never think of their desires. They seek to smother all of their emotions and feelings and literally seek to cease being normal human beings. They become miserable and defeated people. I have the feeling that God is not nearly as concerned with our actions in life as He is our wants. To destroy your wants is to destroy the incentive to live. God gave us the ability to dream.

3. Next we come to our actions. You never get out of the valleys of life by becoming ascetics. Earlier in these pages, I mentioned that I spent one day completely resting in bed. That was a wonderful experience, but two days would have been too much. There comes a time to get up and get going. The ascetic life seems very righteous to

some people. We remember how Peter used the phrase about Jesus as one, ". . . who went about doing good . . ." (Acts 10:38).

We remember that Jesus said, "Therefore whosoever heareth these sayings of mine, and doeth them, I will liken him unto a wise man . . ." (Matthew 7:24). Marvelous power comes into a human life when what we ought to do and what we want to do become pointed in the same direction. The trouble with a lot of us is we are not willing to do what we can do.

One of the greatest stories in the Bible is when Peter and John were going to church one day. As they neared the church a lame man lay there begging. He asked Peter and John for some money. I am sure Peter would have been glad to have rented him a room, bought him some new clothes, paid for his meals, and really taken care of this poor beggar. That would have made the beggar feel good, and it would have made Peter feel good. But Peter said, "Silver and gold have I none." That is where a lot of people would stop. They do not have what they want to give and therefore do not give. However Peter continued, "But such as I have give I thee . . ." (Acts 3:6). When we feel we ought to do something and we feel we want to do something, then we do something. It is as simple as that.

"I Have a Hiding Place"

There is a song that goes, "I have a hiding place, a blessed hiding place." A lot of people can sing that song. It *is* good to withdraw at times, to be alone, to think, to pray, to rest. But we should remember these words, ". . . and Adam and his wife hid themselves from the presence of the Lord God amongst the trees of the garden" (Genesis 3:8). Those were the first two people, and ever since, there have been people seeking hiding places from God, from their duty, from the lives they ought to live. Valleys are the very thing these people are seeking. They do not want to walk *through* the valley; they want to sit down and stay in the valley.

Some of our hiding places are:

1. *Self-induced Sickness.* Physicians have long been saying that a large number of the people who are ill are not really physically sick, but are seeking to escape life. When we "feel bad," not as much is expected of us. A child may not want to go to school some morning

and comes and says to his mother, "I don't feel good this morning." And so it goes in life. This self-induced illness can become very real in our minds. The pain we think we feel can really begin to hurt, until we get to the point where we not only do not expect much of ourselves, but we feel that God does not expect much from us.

2. *The Failure to Decide.* I am told that when one is traveling north through the Archipelago of Southern Alaska, one passes first around Cape Decision before he finds himself at Christian Sound. Your spiritual life is like that, too; you never feel secure until you make that decision.

In my earlier years as a minister, I used to have a tent, and I would go around in the mountains of North Georgia and conduct revivals during the summer. At the close of each service I would give an invitation and talk to people about coming forward and making a decision. I would stop between the verses of a hymn and make further appeals. Often times I would say, "Let's sing a second song, because there is somebody out there trying to decide." I used a lot of pressure to get people to walk down the aisle. At that time our oldest son was about four years old, and driving home one night after a service, he turned to me and said, "Nobody gave you his hand tonight."

I have a feeling that many times God has been disappointed because, "Nobody gave Him his hand." Being able to make up your mind gives you power. Many people hide out from life, with the words, "I just cannot decide."

3. *Refusing to Accept Blame.* One of the classic books of all time is *The Big Fisherman* by Lloyd C. Douglas. In the fourth chapter of that book there is a paragraph which I have marked that I would like to quote again. John the Baptist is speaking:

> "And do I hear you say, 'It is not my fault that the world is wicked; it is the empire that enslaves and robs and kills; am I to be punished for the crime of Caesar?' Then I must answer you that everyone of us is guilty! Do not blame all the injustices, all cruelty, all meanness, on Caesar's empire! For each one of you is a little empire filled with lust and greed and hate! It is easy enough to condemn the government which is, indeed, a rapacious thing that God will cleanse and cleanse

until its bones show through! Easy enough to denounce the Temple for its well-fed lethargy; it deserves and will receive just punishment! But if any peace is to bless this sick world, salvation must first come to you: to you, the lonely shepherd in the hills; to you, the farmer at the plow; to you, the carpenter at the bench; to you, the housewife at the loom; to you, rabbi; to you, lawyer; to you, scribe; to you, majesty. For—except you repent, you shall perish! It is so decreed! God has again spoken! There is one near at hand to rid the world of its inequities! Indeed—He is here now!"

You never win by blaming somebody else for all of your troubles. But this is what people have been doing from the very beginning. Adam ate the forbidden fruit, and he blamed Eve for it. He said to God, "She gave me of the tree, and I did eat" (Genesis 3:12). And we have been blaming each other ever since. Children blame their parents, parents blame the government, and on and on it goes. Emotional maturity means accepting responsibility.

We never get out of the valley until we start walking on our own.

4. *Another emotional hiding place is physical excesses.* The most obvious of these is alcohol. It could be the use of tobacco; it could be eating; some people become what we call workaholics; it could be pleasure and self-entertainment.

Robert Louis Stevenson wrote: "Everybody, soon or late, sits down to a banquet of consequences."

Believe It In

There are many other emotional hiding places, but instead of hiding, there is a better way. In the early nineteen sixties, a reporter interviewed Carl Sandburg and Robert Frost about the idea of building a bomb shelter. After some discussion about the possibilities of the destruction of the world by atomic power, Robert Frost said to the reporter, "Young man, the founding fathers didn't believe in the future. They believed it in." That is wonderful. There is a vast difference in "believing in it" and "believing it in."

When we are in a valley, we not only need to think about in what we believe—we also need to think about what we can believe in.

There are marvelous things ahead, but we need to believe them in. Some eighty years ago, a minister who happened to be a bishop of the United Brethren Church was visiting the president of a small college in the western part of our country. During their conversation, the college president asked the bishop his opinion about the next major advances man would make. The bishop replied that society had now reached its peak and that everything worth inventing had already been produced; he maintained man's material progress was at an end.

The young college president disagreed and said he thought there would be some exciting discoveries in the future. The bishop challenged him, "Name one." The college president replied, "For one thing, I believe that someday men will fly in the air." "Nonsense," the bishop objected, "If God had intended man to fly in the air, He would have given him wings in the first place."

Here we come to the real point of this story. The name of that bishop was Wright. He had two sons, whose names were Orville and Wilbur, and Orville and Wilbur literally believed flying in.

The best things in your life can still come, but you must believe them in.

> I've dreamed many dreams that never came true
> I've seen them vanish at dawn,
> But I've realized enough of my dreams, Thank God
> To make me want to dream on.
>
> I've prayed many prayers when no answer came
> When my hopes and my faith were almost gone
> But answers have come to enough of my prayers
> To make me keep praying on.
>
> I've trusted many a friend that failed,
> And left me to weep alone,
> But I've found enough of my friends true blue
> To make me keep trusting on.
>
> I've sown many seeds that fell by the way
> For the birds to feed upon
> But I've held enough golden sheaves in my hand,
> To make me keep sowing on.

I've drained the cup of disappointment and pain
I've gone many days without a song,
But I've sipped enough nectar from the roses of life
To make me want to live on.

AUTHOR UNKNOWN

Acres of Diamonds

Let me close this section with one of the greatest stories I have ever read. Many years ago there lived in Philadelphia a great minister by the name of Russell H. Conwell, who went all over the nation telling the story entitled *Acres of Diamonds*. With that story he received nearly enough in fees to build the great Temple Baptist Church in Philadelphia and to start the building of the Good Samaritan Hospital there. In addition he was one of the early benefactors of Temple University. This one story served him well. More important it was of great service to those who heard it, learned from it, and acted upon it.

Ali Hafed was living not far from the River Indus in ancient Persia. One day an old priest visited him and among other things told him: "A diamond is a congealed drop of sunlight." The old priest informed him that if he had one diamond the size of his thumb he could purchase the county. If he had a mine of diamonds, he could place his children upon thrones, through the influence of his great wealth. That night Ali Hafed went to his bed a poor man. He had not lost anything, but he was a poor man because he was discontented, and he was discontented because he feared he was poor. He said to himself, *I want a mine of diamonds.* All that night he lay awake thinking, restless.

Early the next morning, he sought out the priest: "Will you tell me where I can find diamonds?" "Diamonds! What do you want with diamonds?" "I wish to be immensely rich, but I do not know where to go." "Well," said the priest, "if you will find a river that runs through white sands, you will always find diamonds." "I do not believe there are any such rivers." "Oh, yes," replied the priest, "there are plenty of them." So Ali Hafed sold his farm, collected his money, and left his family in the charge of a neighbor. Away he went in search of diamonds. He started at the Mountains of the

Moon. Afterwards he came around to Palestine. Then he wandered on into Europe. At last, when his money was all spent and he was in rags, wretchedness, and poverty, he stood on the shores of the Bay at Barcelona, in Spain. A great tidal wave came rolling in between the pillars of Hercules and the poor, afflicted, suffering, dying man could not resist the awful temptation to cast himself into that incoming tide. He sank beneath its foaming crest, never to rise in this life again. But that is not all of the story.

The man who purchased Ali Hafed's farm, one day let his camel into the garden to drink. As the camel put his nose into the shallow water of that garden brook, Ali Hafed's successor noticed a curious flash of light from the white sands of the stream. He pulled out a black stone and took the pebble into the house and put it on the mantel. A few days later, the same old priest came in to visit the man who had purchased Ali Hafed's farm. The moment he opened the drawing-room door, he saw a flash of light on the mantel. He rushed up to it and shouted: "Here is a diamond! Has Ali Hafed returned?" "Oh, no," his friend said, "Ali Hafed has not returned, and that is not a diamond. That is nothing but a stone we found right out here in our own garden." "Yes," said the priest, "but I know a diamond when I see it." Then together they hurried out into the old garden and stirred up the white sands with their fingers and, lo! there came up other more beautiful and valuable gems than the first. An old guide related this story to Dr. Conwell, saying, "Thus was discovered the most magnificent diamond mine in all the history of mankind. Had Ali Hafed remained at home and dug in his own garden or underneath his own wheat field, he would have had diamonds in abundance. For every acre of that old farm has revealed gems which since have decorated the crowns of monarchs."

Most of us feel that if we could just "get out of this valley," all the good things in life would happen to us. It is just possible that the diamonds are right where we are. Somebody has said, "If a fellow isn't thankful for what he's got, he isn't likely to be thankful for what he's going to get." And this friend went on to say, "Life is like an onion, peel it off one layer at a time, and sometimes you weep."

Speaking to a black congregation, Albert B. Cleage, Jr., says in his book, *Black Messiah:*

I ask you to look at all of our black leaders, who suffered and died, and remember one simple fact. It is hard to lead people who are waiting for God to intervene and do everything for them. It is hard to lead people whose basic orientation to struggle is not in terms of what they can do or must do, but rather in terms of God's intervention to do for them what must be done.... When we think of a city called Heaven, do we think of a place for which we must try to possess, to hold, to build, or do we think of something which God is to usher in for us?

14

Slipping Out of Life's Back Door

Why do some people slip out of life's back door? Perhaps the main reason is that they just do not feel worthy of going on. A feeling of lack of worth is one of the most depreciating of all of life's experiences. Many of us feel that the greatest novel ever written is *The Pilgrim's Progress.* When I was a boy, my mother read us that book; through the years I have gone back and reread passages of it. Not long ago I was reading the part where Pilgrim was passing through the valley of humiliation. There he met a terrible character who barred his path. He said to Pilgrim, "Prepare thyself to die; for . . . here will I spill thy soul." I am fascinated by that phrase "here will I spill thy soul." I think that is the only place I have ever seen it used, but it really says something. There are many people whose souls have been spilled. Perhaps the main reason is, one reaches the point of not believing he or she has a soul. There are people who believe life is a prison sentence, that to be born is a crime, that the only cure for birth and life is death. The truth is, and it needs to be emphasized, no person is worthless, and the cure for life is not death but living. Every life is worth living.

One of the people who has inspired me the most was Dr. Pierce Harris. For many years he was pastor of the First Methodist Church in Atlanta, Georgia. I was pastor of Grace Methodist Church in the same city. We lived in the same neighborhood. I cannot count the times my phone rang, and it was Dr. Harris saying, "Charles, meet me out at East Lake Country Club for a round of golf." I would drop just about anything I was doing to get there. I loved to play golf, but to be with him was an even greater experience. We preached together all over the country. My phone rang one night about midnight. It was an announcer at one of the radio stations saying, "Have you heard about Dr. Pierce Harris?" He went on to tell me that Dr. Harris had had an automobile wreck and his dear, lovely wife was killed. Dr. Harris was in the hospital at Eatonton, Georgia. As soon as I hung up I started dressing to go to Eatonton, which was about seventy-five miles away. About two o'clock in the morning I walked into his room in the hospital. He was lying there, looking up at the ceiling. When I came in, he said, "Charles, you should not have come down here tonight." Then after a few moments, he added, "But I knew you would come."

I could never tell all the lessons I learned from Dr. Harris. But I will not forget, one day, he said to me, "When God begins to speak, He always finishes the sentence. There may be a thousand years between the subject and the predicate, but God finally puts down the period."

An example of God "finishing the sentence" begins with the Psalmist saying, "When I consider thy heavens, the work of thy fingers, the moon and the stars, which thou hast ordained; What is man, that thou art mindful of him? . . ." (Psalms 8:3, 4). Through the Psalmist, God asks a question that sooner or later is in the mind and heart of every one of us: When we consider the bigness of this world and this universe, what does one person matter?

More than a thousand years later, God gives us the answer: "As many as received him, to them gave he power to become the sons of God . . ." (John 1:12).

God is mindful of us, not only because of what we are, but because of what we might become. No person is perfect, but every person can live a better life. Every person is of supreme worth. Instead of condemning ourselves for what we are, we should dream of what we might become.

The musical *Man of La Mancha* puts it well:

> To dream the impossible dream,
> To fight the unbeatable foe . . .
> To run where the brave dare not go.
> To right the unrightable wrong . . .
> To try when your arms are too weary,
> To reach the unreachable star!
> This is my quest, to follow that star,
> No matter how hopeless, no matter how far;
> To fight for the right without question or pause,

> To be willing to march into hell
> For a heavenly cause! ...
> And the world will be better for this;
> That one man, scorned and covered with scars,
> Still strove, with his last ounce of courage,
> To reach the unreachable stars.

Again and again, I have walked the streets of Jerusalem and I have seen some of the poverty and hurt of people there. My mind goes back to the first century, when Jesus lived, and I think about the lepers, the beggars, the poor people, and so many who did not have even the common decencies of living. It must have been extremely hard for many people in Jesus' day to maintain a sense of worth and dignity. Not only did they face the hardships of life, but as they walked down the streets they were crowded off by Roman soldiers. There were also many people in Jesus' day who felt scorned by the so-called ruling class. When one is looked down upon, eventually that person has a tendency to look down upon himself.

Yet as Jesus looked at the people of His day He singled out the Samaritans, the harlots, the publicans, the sick people. He did not just tell them that they were good; but as bad as they were, Jesus kept telling them that God cared for them. Consider these words He spoke to people who were "looking down":

> Are not two sparrows sold for a farthing? and one of them shall not fall on the ground without your Father. But the very hairs of your head are all numbered. Fear ye not therefore, ye are of more value than many sparrows.
> Matthew 10:29-31

He told those people God loves them so much that He gave His only Son for them.

Not only did Jesus talk to the people of their worth, He lived in such a way that He demonstrated the dignity of living. When He was spat upon, He did not lose his temper. He never had any money, yet He never thought of himself as poor. He never complained of illness. He healed the illnesses of other people. When nails had been driven through His palms, His love did not turn to hate. Instead He prayed, "Father, forgive them." His dignity never deserted Him.

Jesus made people feel that they were human beings. In giving people a sense of dignity, He helped them avoid doing those things that would make them feel cheap and vulgar.

In contrast there are many people who belittle other people. In belittling others we belittle ourselves. Let me list some of the ways that we depreciate others:

1. We make uncomplimentary remarks about other persons. In this connection think of the advice of John Wesley, who said that when we hear something unkind about another person, let us ask ourselves three questions: Is it true? Is it necessary to repeat it? Is it the loving thing to repeat it?

2. In conversation with others, do we complain about the circumstances of our lives? Self-pity is self-depreciating.

On the other hand, genuine pity for the circumstances of the other person is a marvelous quality. William Saroyan wrote a book entitled *The Human Comedy*. In chapter twenty-six of that book, he said the following, which I copied and have used many times to my own good: "Unless a man has pity he is inhuman and not yet truly a man, for out of pity comes the balm which heals. Only good men weep. If a man has not yet wept at the world's pain he is less than the dirt he walks upon because dirt will nourish seed, root, stalk, leaf and flower, but the spirit of a man without pity is barren and will bring forth nothing— for only pride which must finally do murder of one sort or another—murder of good things, or murder even of human lives."

We depreciate ourselves through self-pity. We exalt ourselves through unselfish pity.

3. Do we make accusations against others, or do we listen to accusations of others?

Every person who wants to be self-respecting should read and study again the story of the woman who was about to be stoned to death because she had violated the law of Moses. When they asked Jesus what they should do, His reply was, ". . . He that is without sin among you, let him first cast a stone at her" (John 8:7).

One by one, those with stones in their hands turned and walked away, until they were all gone. Then Jesus said, "Neither do I condemn thee: go, and sin no more" (John 8:11). Nobody likes to be criticized. I once heard Bishop Gerald Kennedy tell in a sermon how John Ruskin was exceedingly candid in criticizing the art of his friends. He felt that criticism was impartial and should make no difference between real friends.

He wrote to an artist exhibiting a major canvas at the Royal Academy—a very warm, personal friend—saying that he regretted that he could not speak more favorably of the oil painting. "I hope this will make no difference in our friendship," finished Ruskin.

The artist replied by return mail. "Dear Ruskin: Next time I meet you, I shall knock you down; but I hope it will make no difference in our friendship."

Really there is very little difference in making an accusation and in hearing an accusation. We should refuse to hear belittling things about our friends. The person who listens to gossip belittles himself.

4. One of the things we need to be careful about is feeling that we need to constantly explain our actions. That indicates a lack of self-confidence, a lack of self-respect. On the other hand, instead of feeling the need to explain (which shows lack of confidence), one might go to the opposite extreme in loud and excessive boastfulness. Remember Paul said, "Charity vaunteth not itself, is not puffed up" (1 Corinthians 13:4).

Study the people who are really popular with other people. You will find several common traits among them. To begin with, popular people are those who are interested in others. They treat them with respect and courtesy. They are quick to both appreciate and to encourage, and they are very slow to criticize.

More especially we need to be slow to criticize ourselves. We have made mistakes, we have failed, but we need to remind ourselves that mistakes can be corrected—that failure need not be final.

Walt Disney applied at the *Kansas City Star* for a job as an artist. He was told that he did not have talent and was urged to give up art. His first cartoon was *Oswald the Rabbit.* It was a total failure, but after that he drew Mickey Mouse.

In thinking about ourselves, let's remember that greatness comes not "of whom we were born," but "for whom we were born." Greatness comes as we see something to give ourselves to and for. Whoever we are, we can lose our lives in some great cause.

Every so often I find people who have "lost faith." Not having faith in life, it becomes stale and insipid. One of my favorite stories comes from the pen of Lewis Carroll:

"I can't believe that!" said Alice.

"Can't you?" the queen said in a pitying tone. "Try again: draw a long breath and shut your eyes."

Alice laughed. "There's no use trying," she said: "one *can't* believe impossible things."

"I daresay you haven't had much practice," said the queen. "When I was your age, I always did it for half-an-hour a day. Why, some times I've believed as many as six impossible things before breakfast."

Amazing and wonderful things begin to happen as we believe in ourselves.

One way to gain self-respect is to do things that make us feel reverent. There are people who feel that rituals are unimportant. But really rituals are pathways to reverence. I read about an English professor who went to Tibet as a visiting teacher. The first day he entered the classroom, every student in the class stuck his or her tongue out at him. He felt resentful, yet rather than expressing himself, he thought he had better find out what they meant. He discovered that in Tibet sticking out your tongue is a token of respect or a greeting.

An interesting study is human rituals and how they came to be. Once someone asked me the question, "Why do women wear hats in church and men take their hats off?" In the first place, today not even women wear hats, but I had no answer for that. In the Jewish synagogue it is a mark of respect to wear a hat, and it is disrespectful to not wear a hat. Actually there is nothing religious or reverent in either wearing or not wearing a hat.

Religion With Its Shoes Off

In Israel, when we visit a mosque, we take off our shoes and leave them outside. I often wonder why. There is nothing religious about taking off your shoes. But I am reminded of the great experience of Moses. Moses was a fugitive from Pharaoh. He had killed an Egyptian and had fled for his life. Instead of living in a palace, now he was out on the hillside, tending the sheep of his father-in-law, Jethro. He led his sheep to the mountain of Horeb, and then we read:

> And the angel of the Lord appeared unto him in a flame of fire out of the midst of a bush: and he looked, and, behold, the bush burned with fire, and the bush was not consumed. And Moses said, I will now turn aside, and see this great sight, why the bush is not burnt. And when the Lord saw that he turned aside to see, God called unto him out of the midst of the bush, and said, Moses, Moses. And he said, Here am I. And he said, Draw not nigh hither: put off thy shoes from off thy feet, for the place whereon thou standest is holy ground."
>
> Exodus 3:2–5

As we read that story it is marvelous to realize how God could use one person to do what Moses accomplished. After this experience of the burning bush, Moses led the children of Israel out of captivity, through the Red Sea, through the wilderness, and to the border of the Promised Land. He gave the world the Ten Commandments, upon which our civilization is based. It is marvelous how God can use one person.

It is even more marvelous for us to realize that right where we are standing is holy ground and a sacred opportunity. The moment we are now living literally blazes with blessings.

We need to recover our sense of wonder, our anticipation of the glorious, our relationship with something or someone that "turns us on." Thomas Carlyle once said, "The person who cannot wonder . . . is but a pair of spectacles behind which there is no eye." Every one of us needs to retain that something within us that can exclaim, "Wow! Isn't that wonderful!" Too many of us look at life with a mere, "Ho hum." We live in a world of constant miracles. You pick up your phone and talk to somebody on the other side of the world; you can get in an airplane and in a matter of hours fly over the Atlantic, which took Columbus months to cross; you can go to a hospital and see miraculously healed people walking out; you can talk to men in the United States who have literally walked on the moon: miracles are all about us, so much so that we reach the place where they simply do not excite us or inspire us.

Look again at the burning bush that Moses saw. The marvel was that it was burning, but not burning up. Moses was eighty years old, but seeing that burning bush, he got excited. He went there and realized that God was there and that he was standing on holy ground. In our language today he would have said, "Wow! This is glorious!"

So Moses "took off his shoes." Standing in the light of some great inspiration may mean different things for different people. For a Protestant it may be taking off your hat, for a Jew it may mean putting on your hat. For some it may mean taking out your pocketbook, for others it may mean laying aside some smaller duties and giving yourself in a larger enterprise.

"Take off your shoes!" For a person who is defeated, ashamed, feeling that life's opportunities have been missed, it means get up and get going. Moses could have sat on that hillside, watching his sheep and never seeing the burning bush. He took off his shoes, but let us remember he put his shoes back on again; and he marched through the wilderness, up to the top of Mount Sinai and eventually to the border of the Promised Land.

Religion with its "shoes off" is a beautiful, wonderful thing. We go into the House of the Lord with an attitude of reverent respect. However we need to remember that we pull off our shoes in order to put them on again. We become great when we have religion with our "shoes on."

Elizabeth Barrett Browning wrote a poem entitled, "Aurora Leigh." It is a long and difficult poem, but there are four lines that are well remembered:

> Earth's crammed with heaven,
> And every common bush afire with God;
> But only he who sees, takes off his shoes,
> The rest sit round it and pluck blackberries.

Stand in reverent respect before that which inspires you. Feel new strength and power; and then, in the name of the highest and the holiest, get going.

Throughout my ministry I have studied the commentaries written by the great biblical scholar of two hundred years ago, Adam Clarke. On his tomb in Westminster Abbey is a match almost burned out and underneath are these words: "In burning for others, I myself, also, have been consumed."

Some years ago Robert Harrington put on the back of a promotional brochure the words of a dear mother to her son.

> Well, son, I'll tell you:
> Life for me ain't been no crystal stair,
> It had tacks in it,
> And splinters,
> And boards torn up,
> And places with no carpet on the floor
> Bare:
> But all the time
> I've been a climbing on,

And reaching landin's
And turning corners.
And sometimes going in the dark
Where there ain't been no light.
So boy, don't you turn back.
Don't you set down on the steps
Cause you finds it kinda hard;
Don't you fall now
For I'm still goin', honey,
I'm still climbin'
And life for me ain't been no crystal stair.

15

Three of Life's Common Problems

Three of the most common problems we face in making the most of ourselves are these:

1. Being overshadowed by someone else.
2. The fear of old age.
3. The fear of death.

Being Overshadowed

Look at that first problem. One of the men in the Bible who is the most beloved is Barnabas. The Bible says about him, "For he was a good man . . ." (Acts 11:24). There are many reasons why Barnabas was called good, but I think that the main reason was that he was willing to let somebody else get more glory than he got.

Go back and read the story of the beginning of the Christian faith. One of the strongest antagonists of the early Christians was Saul of Tarsus. Later Saul had his conversion experience, and he became known as Paul. However, many of the early Christians were suspicious of him, and perhaps some even held antagonism toward him.

Barnabas was one of the leaders of the church. He was probably the wealthiest man among the early Christians, and he had unusual influence. Barnabas was willing to take Paul as his friend and his co-worker. They started out together as "Barnabas and Paul." However it wasn't long before the great, brilliant Paul emerged as the leader, and later they became known as "Paul and Barnabas."

That is a very difficult experience for many people to bear. To be overshadowed by somebody else makes it hard to keep going. We go to football, baseball, and basketball games, and other athletic events; or we watch them at home on television, and over and over we join in shouting, "We are number one." We see great numbers of people at some sports event holding up one finger and chanting over and over, "One, one, one."

Our society is keyed up for number one, not number two. Recently I was talking with a young man who is a senior in high school. I asked him how he stood in his class, and he told me that he and a girl were tied for first place. I asked who he thought might win out and be the valedictorian of the class. Very disdainfully he said to me, "No girl is going to beat me. I am going to be number one when we graduate." That high-school student has been indoctrinated with that idea, and he probably will carry it the rest of his life. This can be both good and bad. It is good to be a part of the pursuit of excellence, but the fact is, not every person can be number one.

A friend of mine told me a story, and he declared that it was true. A man was elected vice-president of one of the television and radio networks. He was boasting about it to a friend, and his friend laughed at the so-called promotion. He said that being vice-president was meaningless, that companies made vice-presidents of everything. In fact he said there was one big food manufacturer that had a vice-president "in charge of Fig Newtons." He told his friend that if he did not believe it, he could call the company and find out. So his friend accepted the challenge. He called the company, and when the receptionist answered, he said, "I wish to speak to the vice-president in charge of Fig Newtons." The receptionist replied, "Do you mean the vice-president in charge of packaged Fig Newtons or bulk Fig Newtons?" The point is, it is difficult to work as "Paul and Barnabas" if you are Barnabas.

As a young man I became very interested in athletics; that interest has not only remained with me, but has grown through the years. One of the things that I have watched is how on every team there are certain people who are the stars. They are the ones that are watched by the fans, whose pictures are in the paper, and more especially, who draw the fabulously large salaries. The ones that I think about many times are those who practice, who give their best, who work hard but who never are recognized for what they do. The stars could never be stars on any athletic team unless there were some others who were willing to play under the shadow of the athletic heroes. Various sports now have their halls of fame. Every year there are certain ones who are chosen, and every time I read about their elections I think about those who were voted on who did not make it. I wonder how they felt.

There is a man in the Bible whom I have never preached about, and I have never heard anybody else even mention him. His name was Justus. After Judas was gone, the Christians felt it necessary to appoint another apostle in his place. There were 120 Christians at that time, and they decided that there were two persons who were worthy to be appointed: One was Justus and the other was Matthias. They felt each of these men were equally worthy and deserved to be made one of the twelve apostles. But they could not decide which one to select. Not being able to decide, the Bible says that they cast lots. We read, ". . . and the lot fell upon Matthias; and he was numbered with the eleven apostles" (Acts 1:26).

The question I often think about is, *How did Justus feel?* All 120 Christians felt he was worthy, but another man was chosen. Did he keep on working as a Christian? Or did he quit and never come back to another meeting? Nobody will ever know. Really it is hard to keep going when somebody else has been chosen.

I think that one of the greatest people was John the Baptist. We remember that he was at the height of his power and influence when Jesus appeared. John recognized that Jesus was great, and he even said of Jesus, "There cometh one mightier than I after me, the latchet of whose shoes I am not worthy to stoop down and unloose" (Mark 1:7). The crowds left John the Baptist. Even his own disciples forsook him. Jesus became the one they were all following, but John never became bitter or resentful. John the Baptist even said of Jesus, "He must increase, but I must decrease" (John 3:30). It took a great person to do what John the Baptist did.

The name John Allen has great significance for me. That was the name of my brother, just fifteen months younger than I. He and I grew up together, and no two brothers could have loved each other more than we did. The sadness I felt at his death is really indescribable. There was another John Allen, who lived long ago, whom almost nobody has ever heard of. This John Allen was a graduate of Dartmouth. Later he moved west, because of his health, and he settled in Illinois. There he struck up a friendship with a young man in New Salem. He worked with this young man and was his inspiration. They spent many hours together, and he gave direction to his life. Had it not been for John Allen, the world would never have heard of Abraham Lincoln. John Allen stayed in Illinois and saw Lincoln become president of the United States. Sometimes it is hard to remain in the shadows while somebody else has all the glory.

For many years I have been the minister of a large church, and I have received many invitations. But really and truly, I have never been overly impressed by the position one holds or the honors received. Without any doubt, the greatest influence in my life was my own father. He served small churches and received very inadequate salaries. He saw other ministers go far ahead of him. However never did I hear him complain that he was not treated fairly by the church. And today I can honestly say that my greatest ambition in life has been to be a minister like my father. Greatness is not in position. I learned that very early in life. When we are worried about somebody else getting ahead of us, let us remember the words of Jesus who said, "And whosoever of you will be the chiefest, shall be servant of all" (Mark 10:44). Being overshadowed is one of life's valleys that needs to be overcome.

Growing Older

Another valley of life is the aging process. One thing is certain: If we keep living, we are going to keep getting older. Getting older for many people is a depressing experience. It really is one of life's deepest valleys. But age should be one of life's greatest inspirations. Age can bring assurance, satisfaction, and peace of mind that nothing else can bring.

For example consider a teenager: How many years of life does a teenager have? No person can answer that question. The teenager can have a tragic accident or fatal illness. Many things can happen to him. He may live to be twenty or thirty or forty. One never knows. Of course there is some excitement in the adventure of living, but there are also some uncertainties.

When one has lived to be sixty or seventy or even eighty years old, many of the uncertainties are taken away, yet much of the excitement still remains. Instead of wondering if one is going to live in the future, the one who has lived can have the satisfaction of having lived that future.

As a teenager one faces responsibilities and challenges, and that is great, because life would be dull and insipid without mountains to climb. On the other hand, there comes a thrill in standing on the top of a mountain, looking back, and realizing you have climbed it. So it is with age: We can look back over the years and realize we do not have to climb those hills again. I once heard a man say that he was never happier than the day he resigned as general manager of the universe. There comes a time when we do not have to bear all the responsibilities of the world about us.

I identify deeply with the joys of young parents. When a baby comes into a home, the love one feels is thrilling, yet the responsibility that one incurs is awesome. The baby is to be reared, trained, educated, and cared for, and parents feel that responsibility. I went through that experience with my three children, but now I am having great joy in being a grandparent. The truth is, I have advocated that parents should not be allowed to rear their children. I think grandparents should rear them. Grandparents see no fault in their grandchildren. All they feel is that those grandchildren need to be loved and appreciated. I love my grandchildren, and I let their parents do the worrying about them. As far as I am concerned, my grandchildren are perfect in every sense. This is one of the joys that only age can bring.

No one of us can look back and say we have been all that we should have been and done all that we should have done and never made any mistakes. But on the other hand, there comes a time when we need to quit looking back with regret. As I grow older one of the great statements of Paul means more and more to me. I like to read it in the J. B. Phillips translation. It goes like this:

Not that I claim to have achieved all this, nor to have reached perfection already. But I keep going on, trying to grasp that purpose for which Christ Jesus grasped me. My brothers, I do not consider myself to have grasped it fully even now. But I do concentrate on this: I forget all that lies

behind me and with hands outstretched to whatever lies
ahead I go straight for the goal—my reward the honour of
my high calling by God in Christ Jesus.

Philippians 3:12–14 PHILLIPS

Isn't that a marvelous statement, "I forget all that lies behind me
and with hands outstretched to whatever lies ahead. . . ."

Also, as we move along in a hopeful attitude we are not in such a
hurry, and we can really identify with, practice, and experience
these words of some writer who is unknown to me, but whom I appreciate very much:

> Take time to LAUGH, it is the music
> of the soul.
> Take time to THINK, it is the source
> of power.
> Take time to PLAY, it is the source
> of perpetual youth.
> Take time to READ, it is the foundation
> of wisdom.
> Take time to PRAY, it is the greatest
> power on earth.
> Take time to LOVE AND BE LOVED, it is
> a God-given privilege.
> Take time to be FRIENDLY, it is the
> road to happiness.
> Take time to GIVE, it is too short a
> day to be selfish.
> Take time to WORK, it is the price of
> success.
> Take time for GOD, it is the way of life.

If I had the choice, I could very quickly say I would rather "grow
older" than "shrink younger." I can say with my whole heart the
words of Robert Browning:

> Grow old along with me!
> The best is yet to be,
> The last of life, for which the first was made:

Our times are in His hand
Who saith, "A whole I planned,
Youth shows but half; trust God: see all, nor be afraid!"

Death

The third problem people face as one of the real valleys of life is the realization of death. Sooner or later, every person is going to die, and for many people that is a very depressing thought. It is normal to want to live. I am a bit envious when I read that Methuselah became the father of a son when he was 187 years old, that he lived another 782 years after that, and finally died at the age of 969 (Genesis 5:25–27). I confess to you that I have no time set to die. I want to live as long as I can. The tragedy of many people is they start dying before it is necessary.

Many years ago I clipped a poem written by Robert D. Abrahams from the *Saturday Evening Post*. This poem has meant a lot to me, especially as I have grown older. It goes like this:

Tonight Shanghai is burning,
And we are dying too,
What bomb more surely mortal
Death inside of you?
For some men die by shrapnel
And some go down in flames,
But most men perish inch by inch
In play at little games.

From "The Night They Burned
Shanghai"

I personally have no idea how long I will live, but I have determined one thing: I intend to *live* as long as I live! I have a feeling that is one of the greatest resolutions any person can make.

The older I get the more I appreciate the words of Julius Caesar. His friends advised him to take certain measures for the protection of himself. One day he replied to his friends, "He who lives in the fear of death, every minute feels its torture; I will die but once."

In one of his sermons, Dr. Clarence Forsberg, minister of the Missouri United Methodist Church in Columbia, Missouri, tells about Maggie Savoy who was the Women's Editor for the *Los Angeles Times*, until her death in 1975. She died of cancer of the esophagus. In her own words, it was her second time around. Ten years earlier she had undergone surgery for cancer in the abdominal region. She recovered that time, but it struck again. She wanted to write a book to help other people face the ordeal, but she died before the book could be finished. Someone found the raw notes that she had written, and they give us a poignant summary of how she felt and what she wanted to say. These are some excerpts:

Dying is more beautiful the second time around. Not easier. But there is joy to be wrung from the second time. I messed up the first time—my script was flawed, my performance scrawny, resentful, hysterical, and cruel to those I loved and who loved me. I know my lines better now. I know a little more about the art, the craft of dying.

I will not be a symptom-hugger. There are too many in my family. One died in her 90's, still getting her kicks from every headache, backache, bout with lobster, and threatened miscarriage she had fifty years before.

I've learned a lot—practically all of it the hard way—about life and living. I've learned a lot more about dying.

First time around I couldn't find any help. As an outline, one does go through certain steps. They overlap, and not necessarily in order. Disbelief, it can't happen to me, calm, then rage and fury and feeling sorry for yourself.

Somewhere in there comes a heightened sense of ME, and another rage that there will be no ME.

And then, slowly, an entirely new value structure, especially time, possessions, and how to use your energies.

I was lucky I faced my own death, for I have lived more, loved more, accomplished more, BEEN more these last five years than in all the other years put together.

Like the fact of cancer, I have learned another fact. I may not have the choice over what kills me, but I do have a choice over what I kill. I had the power to shape, make, spend, use every single hour still on the books. And I had the power to shape, make, and build love.

These were the only things I owned, the only ME there was. I won't say that it came all at once. I won't say it stayed every time it came. I won't say I don't hate myself for other nights, other rages, other I-am-crying-for-myself excesses.

I do say it as a truth and as a fact. And it profoundly changed our lives. Slowly—like a left-handed kid learns to write—I learned by practice: *One has the power over the quality of one's life.*

The Conclusion

So the conclusion is: there are three valleys that really do not need to be valleys. I can be myself, no matter who somebody else is. I do not have to be worried about being overshadowed by the greater accomplishments of another person. In the second place, I can thank God for age, and instead of it being a valley, it can be a mountain peak upon which I can stand and look out over years of living. In the third place, I cannot choose how long I will live or when I will die, but I can choose the quality of the life I live, and I do not need to live "in the valley of the shadow of death."

"For Thou Art With Me"

16

We Are Not Alone

David wrote the Twenty-third Psalm when he was an old man. He could look back through his life and remember, as a boy, how that he watched over the sheep and how, when they were attacked by a lion or a bear, he protected them (1 Samuel 17:34, 35).

He could remember when he went out to meet Goliath, the Philistine giant who struck fear into the army of Saul. As David faced that giant, he said, "Thou comest to me with a sword, and with a spear, and with shield: but I come to thee in the name of the Lord . . ." (1 Samuel 17:45). David could remember when he became king; he could remember when his dear son died. He could remember experience after experience, but he never reached the place in life where he felt he was big enough that he did not need God. This greatly admired man wrote: "Yea, though I walk through the valley of the shadow of death, I will fear no evil: for thou art with me. . . ."

The truth is, even in the valley of the shadow of death, we keep walking without fear because of His presence. I have seen in many places the wonderful poem "Footprints in the Sand." I understand that it was written by Katharine Simler. Even though it is so familiar to each of us, it helps to remind ourselves of it:

Footprints in the Sand

One night I had a dream—
I dreamed I was walking along the beach
    with the Lord and
Across the sky flashed scenes from my life.
For each scene I noticed two sets of footprints
    in the sand,
One belonged to me and the other to the Lord.
When the last scene of my life flashed before us,

I looked back at the footprints in the sand.
I noticed, that many times along the path
  of my life,
There was only one set of footprints.
I also noticed that it happened at the
  very lowest and saddest times in my life.
This really bothered me and I questioned the
  Lord about it.
"Lord, you said that once I decided to follow you,
You would walk with me all the way,
But I have noticed that during the most
  troublesome times in my life
There is only one set of footprints.
I don't understand why in times when I
  needed you most, you should leave me."
The Lord replied, "My precious, precious child,
  I love you and I would never,
  never leave you during your times of
  trial and suffering.
When you saw only one set of footprints,
It was then that I carried you."

Sooner or later every person reaches the point of the need for companionship. Through the years, I have loved that song:

Me and my shadow,
Not a soul to tell my troubles to;
Just me and my shadow,
All alone and feeling blue.

Loneliness is one of the hardest of all of life's burdens. I have long admired Admiral Richard Byrd and read with interest his adventures in the polar regions. At one point he almost reached the place of desperation; he felt his life nearing its end. His physical strength was almost gone. Later in his book *Alone,* he wrote these words:

I solved it by changing my thoughts. When negative thoughts began to come in my mind, I repulsed them and instead filled my mind with thoughts of the presence of God. Suddenly, I had a feeling of confidence and quietness within. The outer situation was just the same, was just as desperate but it didn't look as difficult, for something had happened inside my mind.

So it is as we walk through the valley; the sense of God's presence gives us power.

There is another little poem that every so often I like to quote. It means a lot to me:

> Don't walk in front of me—
>   I may not follow:
> Don't walk behind me—
>   I may not lead.
> Walk beside me—
>   And just be my friend.

17

"Lord, I Believe"

I love the story of Jesus with Peter and James and John on the mountain when they experienced Jesus' transfiguration. While they were there, Elijah and Moses came from heaven to join Jesus. Here we have an example of God's faithfulness. Moses was denied the opportunity to go into the Promised Land, but God let him come from heaven to visit with the Lord in that land. Eventually Moses *did* set foot in the Promised Land.

Later Jesus and His disciples came down from the mountain, and there they met a father whose son was sick. He brought his child to Jesus to heal. Jesus said to him, "If thou canst believe, all things are possible to him that believeth" (Mark 9:23).

The great accomplishments in life are for the believers. I heard of a teacher in Chicago who would say to his students, "Think of your mind as a motion-picture screen; then put on that screen the picture you want to accomplish. Then take it off and put it on again; then take it off and put it on again, and keep putting that picture on the screen of your mind until it remains there and you can see it." There is marvelous power in fixing pictures in our minds. Ralph Waldo Emerson said, "A man is what he thinks about all day long." Marcus Aurelius put it this way: "A man's life is what his thoughts make of it."

One of the ministers I have most admired is Dr. Norman Vincent Peale. Many years ago, when I was the pastor of a church in a small town in Georgia, I had a wife and three children, and we made barely enough money to live on. I wrote to Dr. Peale and said to him that I would like to come and visit him. Very graciously he wrote me back that he would be happy to see me. I borrowed the money and paid the fare to New York. It was a thrilling experience that day to visit, privately and personally, with Dr. Peale. God gave him a magnetism that is indescribable. He said something to me that day that he has said many times, and I have truly believed it. He said, "Change your thoughts, and you change your world." Many of us believe that America has never produced a more inspiring and effective minister than Norman Vincent Peale.

Those of us who have followed football know that Knute Rockne was one of the greatest coaches America has ever produced. Once he said that there were four rules he followed for the selection of the players on his great Notre Dame teams. Those rules were:

1. I will not have anybody with a swelled head, for you cannot teach him anything.
2. I will not have a griper, kicker, or complainer.
3. I will allow no dissipation.
4. I will not have a boy with an inferiority complex; he must believe he can accomplish something.

Those are not only great rules for a football player; they are great rules for life. The wisest psychologist America ever produced was William James. He said it this way, "Our belief at the beginning of a doubtful undertaking is the one thing that assures the successful outcome of our vision."

However, let us point out the fact that in response, this father of the sick boy said to Jesus, "Lord, I believe." He did not just say, "I believe." I emphasize the fact, he said, "... *Lord, I believe* ..." (Mark 9:23, 24). He put the Lord first.

Likewise, David did not simply say, "Believe you can walk through the valley, and you can do it." He was careful to say, "... For thou art with me...."

America's beloved poetess Helen Steiner Rice, wrote "The Legend of the Spider and Silken Thread Held in God's Hand." I think the poem is wonderful. It goes like this:

> There's an old Danish Legend
>   with a lesson for us all
> Of an ambitious spider
>   and his rise and fall.
> Who wove his sheer web
>   with intricate care

As it hung suspended
    some where in midair,
Then in soft, idle luxury
    he feasted each day
On the small, foolish insects
    he enticed as his prey,
Growing ever more arrogant
    and smug all the while
He lived like a "king"
    in self-satisfied style—
And gazing one day
    at the sheer strand suspended,
He said, "I don't need this,"
    so he recklessly rended
The strand that had held
    his web in its place
And with sudden swiftness
    the web crumpled in space—
And that was the end
    of the spider who grew
So arrogantly proud
    that he no longer knew
That it was the strand
    that reached down from above
Like the chord of God's grace
    and His infinite love
That links our lives
    to the great unknown,
For man cannot live
    or exist on his own—
And this old legend
    with simplicity told
Is a moral as true
    as the legend is old—
Don't sever the "lifeline"
    that links you to
THE FATHER IN HEAVEN
    WHO CARES FOR YOU.

God expects us to do our part.

Notice the wording of the Twenty-third Psalm. Before David says, ". . . for thou art with me . . . ," he says, "Yea, though I walk. . . ." That is, we can depend on God's help, but we also must use our own strengths and do what we can do. Many times we just settle down and expect God to do everything. God expects that we first use the gifts and strengths He has already given us.

Too often we are prone just to think about our weaknesses and forget our strengths. I am the minister of a church located in the center of a large city. Every day people come in seeking help. One day a man came, and I noticed that he had on only one shoe; the other foot was bare. I said to him, "I see you have lost a shoe." He made a marvelous reply. He said, "No, I found a shoe."

I was looking at the bare foot, instead of the foot with the shoe, and that is a tendency many people have in life. God expects us to do what we can and use what we have.

I like the story of a man who, one wintry day, went to traffic court in Wichita, Kansas, not knowing court had been canceled because of a blizzard. A few days later he wrote this letter:

> I was scheduled to be in court February 23rd, at 12:15 P.M., concerning a traffic ticket. Well, I was there as scheduled and to my surprise I was the only one there. No one had called to tell me that the court would be closed, so I decided to go ahead with the hearing as scheduled, which meant that I had to be the accuser, the accused and the judge. The citation was for going 46 miles per hour in a 35 mile per hour zone. I had the speed alert on in my car, set for 44 miles per hour, and as the accuser, I felt that I was going over 35 miles per hour, but as the accused I know that I was not going 46 miles per hour. As judge, and being the understanding man that I am, I decided to throw it out of court this time. But it had better not happen again.

I think there may be times when God expects us to forgive ourselves and not be constantly worrying Him. He has already spread His mercy about us in great abundance.

Speaking of going to court, a young man once phoned me to say that he was in jail. He had no money and asked if I could help him. I went down to the jail and posted bond and got him out. He was guilty of a minor infraction, but it was his first offense, and I was deeply sympathetic. I was given the chance to say a word to the judge. I simply said, "Judge, this is a good boy; he has no record of any previous offense, and I stand here to ask mercy from you."

The judge replied to me, "Dr. Allen, in this court we do not practice mercy, we only practice justice. This boy shall be found guilty." I replied, "Judge, someday you are going before the judgment bar of God, and if God only practices justice, then I want to say to you that you are going to hell."

It's a wonder he did not find me in contempt of court, but he didn't. However I hope I am never a defendant in that judge's court. I have an idea I would not come out very well.

Most of us are not really looking for justice. We are looking for mercy. There are many who feel that the greatest hymn that's ever been written are the words of John Newton:

> Amazing grace—how sweet the sound—
> That saved a wretch like me!

18

The Grace of God

Every person who ever lived on this earth stands in need of the grace of God. In the Bible there are three distinct meanings of grace:

1. *The Forgiving Mercy of God.* ". . . By grace ye are saved," says Paul (Ephesians 2:5). *Grace,* in this connection, means "the unmerited favor, the mercy, the loving-kindness of God." God has two hands: the hand of grace and the hand of judgment. "If we will not take from the hand of grace," said Stanley Jones, "we will have to take from the hand of judgment."

Grace is the ultimate expression of the love of God—the love that is seeking, selfless, suffering, saving, and supreme. As the shepherd searches for his lamb on the dark mountainside, so is God seeking man, though His love was spit back into His face with the words "He saved others; himself he cannot save . . ." (Matthew 27:42). His measureless love continues to climb new Calvaries, knowing that love through suffering will someday save from sin.

Grace might be described as the activity of God's love. As George Matheson expressed it, "O Love that wilt not let me go . . . I give thee back the life I owe. . . ." Once, at the moment of a very difficult decision, David Livingstone said, "I felt the down-reach of the divine." "Though I forget Him and wander away, still He doth love me wherever I stray" we like to sing.

Once a father who had again and again gotten his boy out of trouble, until he had spent all his money and broken his health, finally said, "I had to wash my hands of my boy. What else can I do?" Well, the grace of God is the opposite of His washing His

106

hands of us. His loving mercy, which we do not deserve, is ever pressing in upon us.

Someone has asked, "Whence to the singer comes the song?" Nobody knows. A painter paints an object, a poem is an expression of intelligence. But music is a mystery. Out of the Everywhere comes melody. Music was not invented; it was pressed in upon man's soul.

Likewise, yet more mysterious than music, is our belief in God. Where did the idea of God come from? Certainly man did not just invent it. No one has ever proved God. Man believes in God because he cannot do otherwise. The eye does not create light, rather does light create the eye. Destroy all light and soon the eye would be destroyed. The fish in the dark rivers of Mammoth Cave are an illustration.

Likewise, man's belief and faith do not create the idea of God. Rather does the existence of God create the ability in man to believe and have faith. Just as one can become color-blind (which is the inability to properly interpret the light rays), just as one can become totally blind, so one can become God blind. As we cut ourselves off from God by sin, we "wither away," as Jesus said of the branch, and become incapable of understanding God or feeling God at all.

But by His Grace, God is ever seeking us. Clarence E. McCartney told of a little girl in Scotland who liked to go with her shepherd father and listen as he called the sheep. By and by she grew to womanhood; moved to the city, away from her father; and eventually drifted into wrong that led to despair and loneliness.

Hearing about it, the old shepherd went to the city; but he could not find her. One day he started walking the streets, sounding the shepherd's call loud and free. His daughter's heart suddenly leaped. The call was unmistakable. She rushed out into the street and into her father's arms.

That is the experience we sing about:

> Amazing grace—how sweet the sound—
> That saved a wretch like me!
> I once was lost, but now am found,
> Was blind but now I see.

2. *Strength For Life's Burdens.* The term "thorn in the flesh" sooner or later comes to have meaning for every person. For John Milton it meant blindness; for Alfred, Lord Tennyson it was loneliness; for Jean François Millet it was poverty. For each of us it means something. And like Paul we pray repeatedly that our "thorn" might be removed. Often God does answer as we ask.

On the other hand, God often does something better than removing the thorn. He gives us the grace to bear it. He says, "My grace is sufficient for thee ..." (2 Corinthians 12:9). In that sense, *grace* means "power to overcome."

Here is an example. An oyster is quietly sleeping in the warmth of the sea. A tiny grain of sand is borne along on the current and is caught in the oyster's open shell. An annoyance has entered into the oyster's life; but instead of fighting the intruder, the oyster proceeds to manufacture an exudation of gummy substance, which it spins out around the "thorn in its flesh." Thus the thorn becomes a pearl. "A pearl is a garment of patience which encloses an annoyance."

During World War I, Cardinal Désiré Joseph Mercier's beautiful cathedral was bombed, his priceless books destroyed, and some of his students slain in cold blood. Out of the experience that great man of God wrote: "Suffering accepted and used will give you a serenity which may well prove the most exquisite fruit of your life."

Milton's blindness resulted in *Paradise Lost.* God's grace wrought "In Memoriam" out of Tennyson's loneliness, and *The Angelus* from Millet's poverty. "We shroud the cages of birds," said Jean Paul Ritcher, "when we would teach them to sing." Or as Lloyd C. Douglas put it, "Sometimes God doesn't save us from the storm but in the storm." Grace is the substance God puts around your thorn and of it makes the pearl of life.

I doubt that God ever puts the thorn in our flesh. The very circumstances of life do that. But right off it becomes a blessing because it creates a sense of need. We drop our smugness, we are not as cocky. We begin to feel that we cannot handle life by ourselves. And eventually we reach the point of saying, "Lord, I am not sufficient unto myself. I now yield myself to You. I ask You to receive me, fill me with Thy power, guide my ways." Anything that gives us a sense of the need of God is a blessing.

There is an old hymn by Joseph Hart that pleads:

> Come ye sinners, poor and needy,
> Weak and wounded, sick and sore;
> Jesus ready stands to save you,
> Full of pity, love and power. . . .

I especially like the third verse, which says:

> Let not conscience make you linger,
> Nor of fitness fondly dream;
> All the fitness he requireth
> Is to feel your need of him. . . .

I have never known suffering to be adequately explained. Time and again we have no answer for it. Jesus said: ". . . In the world ye shall have tribulation: but be of good cheer. . . ." What is the rest of that verse? Is it, "I have explained the world"? No, He says, ". . . I have overcome the world" (John 16:33). God's grace does not always explain or remove the thorn, but it is always sufficient to overcome.

3. *Graceful Beauty.* One of the loveliest scenes in the Bible follows Paul's talk to the elders of the church of Ephesus. He had talked about his ministry among them, had bid them good-bye, and they knelt together for a prayer. Then we read, "And they all wept sore, and fell on Paul's neck, and kissed him" (Acts 20:37).

Ordinarily the idea of men kissing another man is repulsive. But not in this instance. As I picture Paul in my mind, I see one who is rough in appearance, wearing cheap and ill-fitting clothes, frail and sickly, with stooped shoulders. He is not at all handsome. Yet there is such a winsome attractiveness about him that he is actually magnetic. He is so lovable that it seems right and proper that even men should want to kiss him.

There is only one explanation. The same thing happened to Paul that happened to the first Christians. We read, ". . . great grace was upon them all" (Acts 4:33). Here *grace* means "charm, beauty, and radiance." It is a marvelous experience for one to become graceful. It means he is poised, harmonious, free of conflict within himself and with other people. The grace of God makes one that way.

Many times my wife, our children, and I visited in the mountains of Georgia and North Carolina. One afternoon we fixed our supper and drove to a spot a few feet more than a mile high. The air felt so clean you wanted to breathe as deeply as possible. The sunshine on the distant peaks seemed like a halo.

We climbed a short way down the mountainside to where a little creek tumbled over a big rock, and there we ate our supper. Food has never tasted so good to me. The stream was clear and cold and as we drank of the water we knew it was pure. In reverent quiet we watched the sun gradually drop out of sight. Even the children talked in subdued tones. The very beauty of the world about us was refreshing. The mountains, the trees, the little creek, and the rocks cast their spell over us, and I realized "great grace was upon them all."

That was God's creation. God does the same thing for people. It is completely indescribable. How can you describe love? How can you describe sunlight? No person can give a definition of beauty. There are some things you cannot hold in your hands; you cannot diagram them; even the senses of hearing and seeing cannot completely take them in. There are some things you can only feel with your very soul.

Who is the most attractive, winsome person you have known? How do you explain that person's attractiveness? Not because of the physical beauty of his or her body. It is an indefinable quality the person possesses. This old apostle was actually ugly, yet as strong men bade him good-bye, "They all wept sore, and fell on Paul's neck, and kissed him." It is unexplainable, yet we understand because we have had like feelings.

A minister friend tells of a rather plain, ordinary girl who stood one day in a meeting to say a few words. She said, "Once there was a man, a wonderful man who prayed under the stars, walked on the roadways, and sat on the hillside. He talked to people, He fed the hungry, He healed the sick. He had a wonderful way about Him.

"Bad men plotted against Him, and one day they hung Him on a cross. When He died, everybody was sad. That was not the end of it. He rose from the dead, and now He lives; and whenever human beings turn to Him, they find Him, and He helps them, and He makes life so wonderful for all of us."

The minister said that as she spoke this plain girl was transformed into a beautiful woman. Her countenance became lighted, her eyes and hair became soft and lustrous. He said, "Now I know what the old artists meant by putting a circle around a head and calling it a halo. Great grace was upon her."

I do not explain it, but I do know God's grace gives to one an undisturbed, calm attitude. The person develops a sense of easygoingness, and he begins to live on a level above petty irritations and exasperations. When God's grace comes into one, he becomes relaxed and controlled. Such a person is easy to know. You are not afraid of him.

There is another illustration of this truth. A lady's dainty handkerchief was ruined by an ugly ink blot. John Ruskin saw it and asked to borrow it for a few days. When he brought it back, where there had been a blot, there was now beauty; for he made the blot the foundation of a lovely design. And the Master does that with the ugly blots on our lives and in our personalities as we become caught up in His purpose.

This is one meaning of the "grace of the Lord Jesus Christ."

Mercy, strength, beauty—no wonder we feel blessed by the benediction: "The grace of the Lord Jesus Christ be with you all" (Revelation 22:21). Those are the Bible's last words.

19

A Letter From God

Some time ago somebody sent me "a letter from God." I do not know who the human author might have been, but as I read this letter I do believe it really could have been written by God Himself.

When we are in the valley and feel hopeless and helpless, let's remember that we are not dependent on our own efforts and our own strengths.

The letter follows:

My dear Child:

My child, I love you! I shed my own blood for you to make you clean. You are mine now; so believe it is true. You are lovely in my eyes and I created you to be just as you are. Do not criticize yourself or get down for not being perfect in your own eyes. This leads only to frustration. I want you to trust me, one step, one day at a time. Dwell in my power and love. And be free . . . be yourself!! Don't allow other people to run you. I will guide you, if you let me. Be aware of my presence in everything. I give you patience, love, joy, peace. Look to me for answers. I am your shepherd and will lead you. Follow only me!! Do not ever forget this. Listen and I will tell you my will.

I love you, my child, I love you. Let it flow from you . . . spill over to all you touch. Be not concerned with yourself . . . you are my responsibility. I will change you without you hardly knowing it. You are to love yourself and love others simply because I love you! Take your eyes off yourself! Look to me! I lead, I change, I make, but not when you are trying. I won't fight your efforts. You are mine. Let me have the joy of making you like Christ! Let me love you!! Let me give you joy, peace and kindness. No one else can!

112

Do you see, my child? You are not your own. You have been bought with blood and now you belong to me. It is really none of your business how I deal with you. Your only comment is to look to me and me only! Never to yourself and never to others. I love you. Do not struggle, but relax in my love. I know what is best and will do it in you. How I want freedom to love you freely! Stop trying to be and let me make you what I want. My will is perfect! My love is sufficient. I will supply all your needs. Look to me, my child.

I love you,
YOUR HEAVENLY FATHER

20

We Need Companionship

When David says that he can walk through the valley, "... for thou art with me...," he is not thinking of God in man's terms. There are times when human companionship and human emotions are important and essential. Many of us can testify that since our spouses died, life has become a different experience. Once a very prominent man received a high honor. Later he said, "The honor really doesn't mean much to me now. My wife died last year, and now I have nobody to tell it to." Having "somebody to tell it to," somebody to walk with, someone to share your feelings, someone to give you support when you need it, having someone to reach out to you, or someone to whom you can "reach out to" means so very much.

Recently I read the following, which is entitled, *Risking*. I do not know who wrote it, but I think it is wonderful.

To laugh is to risk appearing unconcerned.
To weep is to risk appearing sentimental.
To express your independence is to risk losing your friends.
To trust others is to risk being taken advantage of.
To make a decision is to risk making a mistake.
To admit a mistake is to risk losing the respect of others.
To reach out to another is to risk involvement.
To show feelings is to risk exposing your true self.
To place your ideas, your dreams before the crowd
    is to risk their loss.
To love is to risk not being loved in return.
To live is to risk dying.
To hope is to risk despair.
To try at all is to risk failure.

I have wept and appeared sentimental—I have trusted and
been taken advantage of. I have loved and not been loved in
return. But Lord, far better it is to dare ... even though at
times checked with failures, than to live in that gray twilight
of security that does not know that to risk, to love, to care ...
Mainly just to be you, is one of life's greatest treasures ...
that of becoming real.

To try to walk through life without human companionship can be
a very difficult experience. Certainly, it is true we can "walk
through the valley" if there is a friend by our side.

Some time ago I copied this paragraph from *The Unbelonging,* by
Alice M. Robinson:

Most people have a lot of acquaintances—you know, people you meet casually on social occasions, or people you
work with, day in and day out. If something unhappy occurs
with them, you are sorry and you try to help. But—a real
friend? Well, that grows slowly and through lots of trials and
tribulations. I think probably its strongest base is trust. First,
you learn to trust someone, and from that point on, you care
very much what happens to them. Even when they are very
far away, you care, and you want to know how they are, and
what they are doing and like. You share things—good and
bad—with your real friends and you feel comfortable with
them.

For many years I have spent my life living in a city. Many of my
friends have places down on the beach, out on a lake, or in the
woods or the mountains someplace. They are beautiful places, and
one can dream of being quiet and being alone. I know many who
have sold their homes in the city when they retired and have moved
to some remote area. But that does not appeal to me. When I retire,
I want to live among people.

One of America's greatest ministers of the last generation, and
one of my good friends, was Dr. George A. Buttrick. He once
quoted Emerson: "Every man passes his life in search of friendship.

Our chief want is somebody who shall make us do what we can. That is the service of a friend."

Then Dr. Buttrick goes on to comment: "I read the other day of a homespun statement of the same truth. Old Maggie had been for years very frequently in her cups. She was sent to the country so that in quietness and away from temptation she might find healing. But she found no healing, and soon she was back in the city in her former haunts. Why had she not been content to live among the trees? she was asked. Her reply was, 'People is better than stumps!' "

The person who shuts him or herself away from the companionship of other people is making a great mistake. There are many ways and many places one can find companionship of friendly people. The point is to seek out those places and take the initiative. One day Carl Kopf, the author, was watching police grappling for the body of a person who had jumped from Harvard Bridge. Someone asked why the woman had jumped. Kopf ventured: "Maybe she had no work and nothing to eat. Maybe she had no friends and was lonely." The person replied, "Well, she won't find any friends in the river." If you expect to find friends you must go where people are.

There are few people who want to live alone the way Jonathan Swift described in this little poem:

> We are God's chosen few,
> All others will be damned;
> There is no place in heaven for you,
> He can't have heaven crammed.

21

We Need Friends, and We Think of God as a Friend

We read, "And the Lord spake unto Moses face to face, as a man speaketh unto his friend..." (Exodus 33:11). Truly God is a friend, but we need to know God is not the same as an earthly friend or an earthly person. There are persons who seek to think of God within man's limits. We hear the phrase "the man upstairs." That is utterly ridiculous, because there is no "man upstairs." Our God does not have human limitations.

The anthropomorphic approach thinks of a God who is a very old person with a long, flowing robe and a white beard. It is difficult for us to understand how, even if God were a superman, He could know every person on earth. The point is, God is utterly beyond our comprehension. He is so great that He can make a planet or a universe just as easily as He can cause a little violet to grow. God is concerned with each one of His people. As we read the Bible, as we read history, over and over again, we find God dealing with individual persons. Many people say with the great Charles H. Spurgeon, "I looked at God and He looked at me, and we were one forever."

"... for Thou art with me..." eliminates the impossibility of any valley. God is not with us just if we are good or on certain days or in certain periods. God is faithful *all* the time. Somebody wrote a poem entitled, "If God Should Go On Strike."

It's just a good thing God above has never gone on strike.
Because he wasn't treated fair on things he didn't like.
If he had only once sat down and said "That's it—I'm through!
I've had enough of those on earth, so this is what I'll do.

I'll give my orders to the sun, cut off the heat supply
And to the moon, give no more light and run your oceans dry.

117

Then, just to really make it tough and put the pressure on,
Turn off the air and oxygen till every breath is gone!"

Do you know he would be justified if fairness were the game.
For no one has been more abused or treated with disdain

Than God—and yet he carried on supplying you and me
With all the favors of his grace and everything—for free.

Men say they want a better deal and so on strike they go,
But what a deal we've given God whom everything we owe.

We don't care who we hurt or harm to gain the things we like
But what a mess we'd all be in if God should go on strike!

22

The Consecration of Sorrow

In the year 1912 Dr. Cleland McAfee wrote an editorial for a publication called *The Continent*. The title of that editorial is "The Consecration of Sorrow." Even though these words are nearly seventy years old, they truly and beautifully express our feelings today.

The most puzzling question which comes to Christian people at a time of great sorrow is, Why? There is little use in telling us that we ought not to ask it. It is true we may not be able to find a full answer, yet there is more answer than we find, for most of us look for it in the wrong place. We look back to find what precedes our experience to learn the reason which God had in letting us have it. The best reasons for God's greatest deeds, so far as we know them, lie after the deeds themselves. Most of us will find the best answer to our question by looking forward. . . .

The greatest experience must have the greatest reasons. When we find ourselves maimed and broken, we get no comfort in looking back and seeing that it was our fault or that it might have been different if we had done this or that. Constant brooding on the irrevocable is useless. Here is the experience, whatever was the cause of it. No matter if we see a thousand things that might have changed this, it cannot now be changed. Very well, then, what shall we do with it in the days that are coming? Since we cannot see God's reasons behind us, let us work His reasons out in the days that are before us. Let us learn the secret of the consecration of our sorrow. Whatever it was that made the sorrow, nothing can be half so important as what the sorrow can make of us.

You have lost someone very dear to you and you are completely staggered by it. Friends suggest reasons why God

allowed this sorrow to come to you. The reason may not lie
behind you at all but altogether before you. It may lie in the
future of your loved one. It may lie in the future of your own
heart. It is absolutely sure that God means the sorrow to do a
great thing for you. You are to be more efficient in life than
you would have been without that sorrow. You will be more
efficient if you will consecrate it. If you let it shut you in from
the world so that you grow indifferent to the world's great
sorrow, you have done the loving Father an injustice. That
sorrow opened a path straight from your feet out to the
needy world. You cannot turn from that path without losing
the best reason for its being opened.

You can consecrate this sorrow. You know better now
what loads are, and what disappointments are, and what
failure is. For one reason and another the world is full of all
these things. You are one of God's marked people hereafter,
for you have passed through an experience that has in it the
making of might. Keep your eyes forward; never mind what
preceded the trouble. Be very sure that God's richest reason
lies in what He and we together can make of the experience
He gives us.

23

I Feel the Need to Say Something Like This . . .

Thinking of the valleys of life and thinking about companionship—both human and divine—when we are in that valley, we feel the need to say something like this:

God hath not promised
Skies always blue.
Flower-strewn pathways
All our lives through.
God hath not promised
Sun without rain,
Joy without sorrow,
Peace without pain.

But God hath promised
Strength for the day.
Rest for the labor.
Light for the way,
Grace for the trials,
Help from above,
Unfailing sympathy,
Undying love.

ANNIE JOHNSON FLINT

24

God's Psychiatry

Some years ago I wrote a book entitled *God's Psychiatry*. That book has now been published in many languages and year by year has a large sale. In that book I pointed out that the word *psychiatry* really comes from two Greek words, *psyche* and *iatreia: psycheiatria.* The word *psyche* means the core of a person's being and is variously translated as "breath," "soul," "mind," "reason," and the like. The word *iatreia* means "treatment," "healing," "restoring," and the like. So, put the two words together and we have "the healing of the mind," or, as David might have said, "the restoring of the soul."

That book was written for people who need their souls healed, people who are in the valley; the first section is based on the beloved Twenty-third Psalm. There I told about a man who came to me in a very disturbed state of mind. I pointed out that had he been physically sick and gone to a physician, the doctor would have examined him and given him a prescription. So after counseling, I took a sheet of paper and wrote out my prescription for him. I prescribed the Twenty-third Psalm five times a day, for seven days. I urged him to take it just as I prescribed it. As soon as he got up in the morning, before he ate breakfast or did anything else, he was to read that Psalm carefully, meditatively, and prayerfully. Then immediately after breakfast he was to do exactly the same thing. He was to read it again after his lunch, after dinner, and finally the last thing before he went to bed. It was not to be a quick, hurried reading. He was to read it slowly, carefully, and soak up as much of the meaning as possible. I promised him that at the end of one week, he would have strengths he never before had; he would see things differently; he would feel healed.

That book was published in 1953, twenty-eight years ago. During the years, it has sold more than a million copies, perhaps even 2 million copies. Every year a lot of people buy that book.

When I wrote *God's Psychiatry,* I believed what I was writing. During these years I have received not hundreds of letters, but literally thousands of letters from people all over the world, saying to me that they were in a valley of life; they took the seven-day prescription of the Twenty-third Psalm, and it has been a tremendous and powerful blessing in their lives.

For people who are "walking through some valley," I most enthusiastically prescribe the Twenty-third Psalm. No person need be defeated by the valley.

I quote a little poem that has meant a great deal to me, and I send to all in a valley:

> Bring me a rose in the wintertime
> When a rose is hard to find.
> Bring me a rose in the wintertime
> I've got roses on my mind.
> For a rose is sweet
> Most anytime, and yet,
> Bring me a rose in the wintertime
> It's so easy to forget.

ANONYMOUS

Caution
God Doesn't
Look for
Trophies. He
Looks for Scars.

CHRISTIAN HERALD ASSOCIATION AND ITS MINISTRIES

CHRISTIAN HERALD ASSOCIATION, founded in 1878, publishes The Christian Herald Magazine, one of the leading interdenominational religious monthlies in America. Through its wide circulation, it brings inspiring articles and the latest news of religious developments to many families. From the magazine's pages came the initiative for CHRISTIAN HERALD CHILDREN'S HOME and THE BOWERY MISSION, two individually supported not-for-profit corporations.

CHRISTIAN HERALD CHILDREN'S HOME, established in 1894, is the name for a unique and dynamic ministry to disadvantaged children, offering hope and opportunities which would not otherwise be available for reasons of poverty and neglect. The goal is to develop each child's potential and to demonstrate Christian compassion and understanding to children in need.

Mont Lawn is a permanent camp located in Bushkill, Pennsylvania. It is the focal point of a ministry which provides a healthful "vacation with a purpose" to children who without it would be confined to the streets of the city. Up to 1000 children between the ages of 7 and 11 come to Mont Lawn each year.

Christian Herald Children's Home maintains year-round contact with children by means of an *In-City Youth Ministry.* Central to its philosophy is the belief that only through sustained relationships and demonstrated concern can individual lives be truly enriched. Special emphasis is on individual guidance, spiritual and family counseling and tutoring. This follow-up ministry to inner-city children culminates for many in financial assistance toward higher education and career counseling.

THE BOWERY MISSION, located at 227 Bowery, New York City, has since 1879 been reaching out to the lost men on the Bowery, offering them what could be their last chance to rebuild their lives. Every man is fed, clothed and ministered to. Countless numbers have entered the 90-day residential rehabilitation program at the Bowery Mission. A concentrated ministry of counseling, medical care, nutrition therapy, Bible study and Gospel services awakens a man to spiritual renewal within himself.

These ministries are supported solely by the voluntary contributions of individuals and by legacies and bequests. Contributions are tax deductible. Checks should be made out either to CHRISTIAN HERALD CHILDREN'S HOME or to THE BOWERY MISSION.

Administrative Office: 40 Overlook Drive, Chappaqua, New York 10514
Telephone: (914) 769-9000

Allen, Charles
    Victory in the Valleys
    of Life

DATE	BORROWER'S NAME	PHONE NUMBER